Gender, Sexuality, and Body Politics
in Modern Asia

Key Issues in Asian Studies, No. 1
AAS Resources for Teaching About Asia

Gender, Sexuality, and Body Politics in Modern Asia

Michael G. Peletz

Association for Asian Studies, Inc.
1021 East Huron Street, Ann Arbor, MI 48104 USA
www.aasianst.org

MICHAEL G. PELETZ is Professor of Anthropology at Emory University. Professor Peletz's specialties include social theory, gender, sexuality, kinship, law, religion (especially Islam), and modernity, particularly in Malaysia, Indonesia, and other parts of Southeast Asia and the Pacific Rim. He is the author of *Islamic Modern: Religious Courts and Cultural Politics in Malaysia* (Princeton, 2002), *Reason and Passion: Representations of Gender in a Malay Society* (California, 1996), *A Share of the Harvest: Kinship, Property, and Social History among the Malays of Rembau* (California, 1988), and *Gender Pluralism: Southeast Asia since Early Modern Times* (Routledge, forthcoming). He is also the co-editor, with Aihwa Ong, of *Bewitching Women, Pious Men: Gender and Body Politics in Southeast Asia* (California, 1995).

Published by:
Association for Asian Studies, Inc.
1021 East Huron Street
Ann Arbor, Michigan 48104 USA
www.aasianst.org

Library of Congress Cataloging-in-Publication Data

Peletz, Michael G.
    Gender, sexuality, and body politics in modern Asia / by Michael G. Peletz.
        p. cm. -- (Key issues in Asian studies ; no. 1) (Resources for teaching about Asia)
    Includes bibliographical references.
    ISBN 978-0-924304-50-7 (pbk. : alk. paper) 1. Body, Human--Social aspects--Asia.
    2. Body, Human--Political aspects--Asia. 3. Sex role--Asia. 4. Sex customs--Asia. 5.
    Gender identity--Asia. 6. Asia--Social life and customs. I. Title.
    GN625.P45 2007
    306.095--dc22

                                                                    2007024088

ABOUT—Gender, Sexuality, and Body Politics in Modern Asia

"Gender, Sexuality, and Body Politics in Modern Asia" addresses topics of the highest significance for multiple disciplines—anthropology, sociology, gender studies, Asian studies, religion, geography, political science, and history.

This engagingly written booklet—designed for use in undergraduate humanities and social science courses, as well as by advanced high-school students and their teachers—has great potential for use in the classroom, encouraging debate and discussion. It will also appeal to specialists in the field owing to Peletz's ability to present sophisticated yet accessible discussions of a broad range of topics.

Drawing on the vast body of scholarship of those who have either grown up in the region or have spent many years engaged in anthropological fieldwork or other research, Peletz provides a masterful overview of gender, sexuality, and body politics in modern Asia, presenting multiple perspectives in an accessible, jargon-free style.

The "Suggestions for Further Reading" section at the back of the booklet provides students and scholars with a comprehensive guide for further research.

ABOUT—Key Issues in Asian Studies

"Key Issues in Asian Studies" is a series of booklets engaging major cultural and historical themes in the Asian experience. "Key Issues" booklets complement the Association for Asian Studies teaching journal, *Education About Asia*, and serve as vital educational materials that are both accessible and affordable for classroom use.

"Key Issues" booklets tackle broad subjects or major events in an introductory but compelling style appropriate for survey courses.

This series is particularly intended for teachers and undergraduates at two- and four-year colleges as well as advanced high school students and secondary school teachers engaged in teaching Asian studies in a comparative framework.

For further information about "Key Issues in Asian Studies" booklets or about the Association for Asian Studies, please visit www.aasianst.org.

Contents

Acknowledgments

Much of this booklet was written during the 2005–2006 academic year, which I had the good fortune of spending at the Institute for Advanced Study in Princeton. I am grateful to the Institute for financial support (some of which derived from the National Endowment for the Humanities) and for the stimulating intellectual environment that facilitated work on this and other projects. Colleagues at the Institute, at Emory University, and elsewhere provided helpful comments on an earlier draft of this booklet. I would particularly like to thank Carol Gluck, Ann Gold, Robert Hefner, Susan Henry, Drege Byung'chu Kang, Bruce Knauft, Tamara Loos, Barbara Miller, David Nugent, Joan W. Scott, Nancy Smith-Hefner, and anonymous reviewers for their suggestions and other remarks. I am also grateful to Amaris Crawford for her valuable research assistance. Thanks, finally, to Robert Entenmann for commissioning this work, to Ellen Walker for drawing the maps, to Jan Opdyke for copyediting, and to Gudrun Patton and Jonathan Wilson of the Association for Asian Studies for providing assistance along the way. Any remaining errors and shortcomings are of course my own.

Note on Spelling and Transliteration

Throughout this booklet I introduce various Asian-language terms, which I render in italics and spell in accordance with the most current conventions followed by scholars working in the languages in question. For ease of reading and to simplify the booklet's production, I have not used diacritics in my transliteration of Asian-language terms.

1

Introduction

As we enter the new millennium, it may no longer be the case that mention of Asia in Western circles evokes images of bound feet, geisha, the Kamasutra, the immolation of widows, or any of the other kinds of "oriental" difference ("excess," "irrationality") that so preoccupied observers from the Victorian era through the Cold War. Still, for many Westerners Asia remains largely unknown and frequently misunderstood, a land of recurrent natural disaster, frightening contagion, ruthless despotism, and slavish conformity, a source of abundant, cheap labor and home to exotic, compliant (sometimes veiled and secluded) women, unmanly men, and hypermasculine icons such as Bruce Lee and Jackie Chan. Many Western stereotypes of Asia are still heavily gendered and sexed; they are, quite literally, embodied. One of the chief objectives of this booklet is to encourage critical rethinking of conventional wisdom in these areas by offering fresh insights into dynamics of Asian genders and sexualities from the perspective of the social sciences in general and of sociocultural anthropology in particular.

The primary aim of this booklet is to provide college students, teachers, and scholars with an overview of genders, sexualities, and body politics in modern Asia based on the recent scholarship of those who have either grown up in the region or spent many years there engaged in extensive research. It is designed for use at the college level, mainly in undergraduate courses, though it could also be utilized by advanced high school students, their teachers, and others interested in the subject. The booklet may be assigned in courses dealing with one or another region of Asia, or Asia in its entirety, either as the sole source of information on gender and sexuality in Asia or in conjunction with one or more specialized texts on the topic. Because it is, by design, quite short, the booklet must of necessity deal in broad strokes with a range of issues and debates that merit more extensive treatment than is possible here. Readers may find it helpful to consult the bibliography for additional sources as well as the section "Suggestions for Further Reading."

This booklet deals with most but not all regions of Asia. The English-language term "Asia," which derives from a Greek term of the same spelling, generally refers to that portion (roughly four-fifths) of the continent of Eurasia that lies to the east of the Red Sea, the Bosporus Straits at Istanbul, and the

Ural Mountains in the former Soviet Union (see Maps 1 and 2). The focus in this booklet is on three vast areas of Asia now conventionally designated as South Asia, East Asia, and Southeast Asia. Based on geography, climate, and widely distributed cultural complexes, scholars have sometimes referred to this vast expanse as "monsoon Asia." This expansive region is "set off from the rest of Asia by high mountain ranges along most of its landward borders," which are partly responsible for the relatively heavy seasonal winds and rains that affect much of the area (Murphey 1996:2). But since sizable areas of monsoon Asia (e.g., northern China) have no monsoons and do not share in the broadly defined cultural patterns held to be characteristic of much of the rest of the region, I prefer not to use the term.

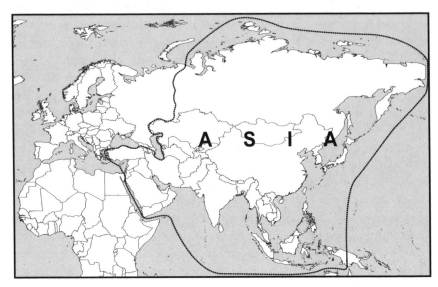

Map 1. Asia

The area that is conventionally designated as South Asia, and sometimes referred to as (or treated as more or less synonymous with) the Indian subcontinent, includes Pakistan, India, Nepal, Sri Lanka, and Bangladesh. East Asia consists mainly of Greater China (the People's Republic of China as well as Taiwan) and the nation-states of North Korea, South Korea, and Japan. The third region of Asia examined here is Southeast Asia, which includes the eleven countries that are situated south of China and east of India: Vietnam, Laos, Cambodia, Thailand, Burma (Myanmar), Malaysia, Singapore, Brunei, Indonesia, East Timor, and the Philippines. The physical and cultural boundaries of these nation-states, like most others — to say nothing of Asia as a whole—tend to be quite porous. More generally, one should not assume that geopolitical boundaries coincide with the borders of broadly defined "culture areas," or that terms as expansive as "Asia" and "Asian" can "designate readily identifiable, coherent categories of characteristics, societies, or individuals" (Vervoorn 2002:2). In this view, "Asia" refers to "a geopolitical region, . . . a loosely delineated part of the world's surface containing a number of different countries and cultures . . . [and] is just a shorthand way of saying 'Afghanistan, Bangladesh, Cambodia, China' and so on" (3).

Excluded from the discussion are Southwest Asia, more commonly known as the Middle East, and North Asia, which encompasses Central Asia and includes Afghanistan as well as Kazakhstan, Turkmenistan, and other parts of the former Soviet Union. In the pages that follow, I use "Asia" as a shorthand term for South, East, and Southeast Asia unless otherwise noted. Most of my comments focus on the lowland areas of Asia where the vast majority of Asians reside; limitations of space do not permit adequate coverage of Asia's highland regions, which are home to numerous ethnic minorities. I should also make clear that, since this booklet has been designed

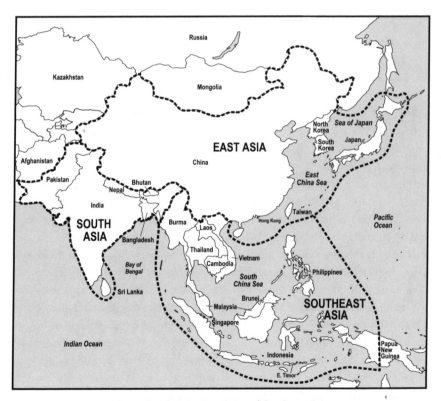

Map 2. South Asia, East Asia and Southeast Asia

for use in English-medium classrooms, I have drawn on publications in English and, with a few exceptions, have not cited Asian-language sources, some of which take different approaches and privilege different concerns and themes.

A final caveat concerns the fact that some of my discussions involve exploration of topics that are iconically associated with certain locales: the sex industry in Thailand, household enterprise in Japan, the intrusiveness of the state in Singapore, communal violence in South Asia (Appadurai 1986). It will be evident in due course that in exploring topic-locale icons such as these I am not suggesting that the skin trade occurs only in Thailand, that family firms exist only in Japan, or that similar kinds of essentializing stereotypes have any conceptual or analytic purchase. Virtually all of the subjects dealt with in this booklet could be examined in the context of a single Asian country. Because this is neither feasible nor desirable in a project of this sort and because some subjects have been better studied in certain regions than in others, I build on the strengths of the available scholarship and offer a portrait of gender, sexuality, and body politics in modern Asia in the form of a mosaic that is designed to fit topical pieces and locales together, albeit without any assumption that these mappings are primordial or exclusive. Mosaics of different design are certainly possible.

Our knowledge of genders and sexualities in modern Asia (and elsewhere) has been shaped by scholars from a number of different academic disciplines, particularly women's studies, anthropology, sociology, history, sexuality studies, gay and lesbian studies, and queer studies. The majority of scholars agree on many basic issues, for example, that political, economic, demographic, and cultural (including religious) variables go a long way toward explaining variation in the structure and organization of gender roles and gender ideologies both historically and cross-culturally; that, for political, economic, and other reasons, systems of male dominance and gender inequality are exceedingly widespread (some would say virtually universal); and that to the best of our knowledge matriarchies, defined as societies ruled by women, have never existed in the past and do not exist at present. But scholars part company on other key issues. Some of the more spirited debates, which I will not rehearse here, focus on how best to define and conceptualize gender, sex, and sexuality. Suffice it to note that some of the disagreements attest to the fact that certain of the fields that are centrally involved in the debates are of relatively recent origin and have changed rapidly since their inception; that the study of gender and sexuality has often been marginalized by research agendas that did not address the questions that have come to be of major concern in recent decades; and that many of the debates have far-ranging political implications and for these and other reasons have become deeply politicized.

It is revealing that through the mid–twentieth century the only entries that many English-language dictionaries included under the heading of "gender" were those that pertained to a feature of grammar. In its grammatical sense, gender refers to the ways nouns, pronouns, and so on are grouped, inflected, and otherwise changed in form according to how they are "gendered" or defined as masculine, feminine, or neuter (assuming that the language designates neuter as a gendered category). French and German provide interesting European examples in light of the different ("opposite") genders they assign to the same basic nouns. In French the word for "sun" (*le soleil*) is masculine while the word for "moon" (*la lune*) is feminine; in German these gender designations are reversed, with the term for "sun" (*die Sonne*) being feminine and the term for "moon" (*der Mond*) masculine. Obviously there is nothing inherent ("natural" or "God-given") in the sun or moon that results in its being gendered one way or the other. The same is true for most other nouns in French and German, which is one reason why it is often difficult for students studying French and German as second languages to learn their gendered dimensions. The case of French, which includes a dual-gender system of classification, is less complex than that of German and Latin, both of which group nouns according to a tripartite scheme of masculine, feminine, and neuter. The English language, by contrast, does not utilize gender in any of these ways, although much of the speech of English-language speakers is nonetheless implicitly gendered.

These linguistic examples illustrate that there is much variation from one language to the next with respect to the specifics of gender (e.g., the particular phenomena that are defined in a given language as masculine or feminine) as well as the numbers of genders utilized in language (two in French, three in German and Latin), and the extent to which gender is a marked feature of language (as in the cases of Latin, French, and German but, comparatively speaking, not English). These and related observations bearing on gender in its linguistic sense are highly pertinent to the other definitions of gender that one is likely to encounter in a dictionary, which are more directly relevant to us. More to the point, cultural constructions of femininity and masculinity are as variable and arbitrary as the assignment of gender in language.

For our purposes, the term "gender" designates the cultural categories, symbols, meanings, practices, and institutionalized arrangements bearing on at least five sets of phenomena: (1) females and femininity; (2) males and masculinity; (3) androgynes, who are partly male and partly female in appearance or of indeterminate sex/gender, as well as intersexed individuals, also known as hermaphrodites, who to one or another degree may have both male and female sexual organs or characteristics; (4) the transgendered, who engage in practices that transgress or transcend normative boundaries and are thus by definition "transgressively gendered"; and (5) neutered or unsexed/

ungendered individuals such as eunuchs. "Sex," by contrast, refers to physical activities associated with desire, reproduction, and the like, including, but not limited to, sexual intercourse of a heterosexual nature; to physical bodies that are distinguished by having genitals that are construed as "female," "male," both (as with some intersexuals), or neither (as in the case of some eunuchs); and to bodily processes associated with anatomical and physiological maturation such as menstruation and ejaculation. "Sexuality," for its part, "may overlap with sex and gender, but . . . pertains specifically" to the realm of erotic desire, passion, and pleasure (Robertson 1998:17).

Every society has a system of "gender roles," defined as behavioral patterns or expectations that are keyed to gender, and a "gendered division of labor," which assigns some tasks and more encompassing activities to males and others to females (and in earlier times was referred to as a sexual division of labor). All such phenomena vary a great deal not only through space (from one society to the next) but also through time (historically). Every society also has a gender ideology, even if it is only implicit. In most, if not all, societies, there are a number of different ideologies or discourses of gender, as Sherry Ortner (1996) points out, although one of them is typically dominant or hegemonic vis-à-vis the others. A "gender ideology" is a set of concepts that specifies the "proper" ("God-given" or "natural") activities, roles, and interrelationships of males, females, androgynes, the transgendered, and so on in accordance with cultural assumptions concerning the "innate" or "essential" similarities and differences among these categories. Gender ideologies encode differences in the prestige (status, honor, esteem) accorded to them and are typically grounded in religious (or scientific) understandings of what is "natural" and morally appropriate for different categories of social actors. One final set of terminological and conceptual points concerns the importance of recognizing that prestige is not the same thing as power (the ability to command the actions of others, an ability that may or may not be construed as legitimate), authority (the ability to exercise power in legitimate ways), or autonomy and social control, which have to do with an individual's ability to exercise agency with respect to the self and others. In the discussion that follows, I focus more on prestige and authority than on power or social control, though I am ultimately concerned with the interactions among these and attendant variables.

I have organized this booklet into five chapters. Chapter 2, "Dynamics of Gender and Sexuality," follows this introduction and offers readers a broad overview of patterns of gender and sexuality in modern Asia. This section (the longest in the booklet) furnishes context for later discussions and a much wider range of topics and locales beginning with more traditional(ized) subjects in anthropology such as the importance of myth, ritual, and religion in providing the implicit frames of meaning through which people understand and experience many aspects of gender and sexuality, both "traditional" and "modern." This section thus encompasses a consideration of the significance of ritual and religion in constructions of gender and sexuality; a comparative exploration of gender ideologies; analyses of gendered experiences in households, families, and factories, including dynamics involving the favoring of sons and discrimination against daughters; and an examination of the cultural politics of weddings and the reasons why romance has emerged as a "national security issue" in some Asian settings.

Chapter 3, "Bodies, Pleasures, and Desires: Transgender Practices, Same-Sex Relations, and Heteronormative Sexualities," addresses themes of gender and sexual diversity both across and within specific Asian societies, demonstrating not only what is taken to be "normal" (normative) in a broad range of Asian contexts but also the fluidity, permeability, and pluralism long typical of many Asian systems of gender and sexuality. Case studies presented in this chapter illustrate some of the divergent (and for some readers unexpected and perhaps surprising) ways in which genders, sexualities, and bodies are aligned and combined in "traditional" as well as "modern" contexts.

Chapter 4, "Bodies on the Line," deals with how bodies, genders, and sexualities are implicated in militarization, warfare, global tourism, prostitution, the AIDS epidemic, and social activism in an age of global connection.

Chapter 5, "Conclusion," provides a summary overview of some of the commonalities in the region and raises a series of questions about possible scenarios for the future.

2

Dynamics of Gender and Sexuality

Students and scholars who seek to understand the variegated norms, forms, and experiences of gender and sexuality in contemporary Asia face a potentially bewildering range of diversity. But they quickly discern underlying commonalities, especially among the majority, who adhere to one or another of the world religions and live in (or come from) lowland areas given over to the cultivation of grains such as rice. The diversity exists partly because the peoples of Asia, who currently number about four billion and thus comprise over 60 percent of the world's population, are distributed throughout all of the climatic and ecological zones found on the planet, each of which imposes its own set of constraints on human populations, their ways of making a living, and the social structures and institutions that give form and meaning to people's lives. Asia is also the birthplace of many world religions—including Hinduism, Buddhism, Sikhism, Confucianism, and Taoism (as well as Judaism, Christianity, and Islam if one considers Asia in the broad sense of the term)—the doctrines of which are quite distinct from one another with regard to gender, sexuality, and much else. Further complicating the situation are differences in the historical development of these religions, including contrasts in the ways they spread throughout the region and interacted with the local religious systems (involving feasting, animal sacrifice, the propitiation of local spirits, etc.) that they encountered. Asians' historical experiences—of colonialism, imperialism, war, and revolution, for example—along with the structures of governance that currently exist in Asia, vary widely as well, even though monarchies, feudal arrangements, and local polities of various stripes have for the most part been replaced or superseded either by systems of democracy or by institutionalized arrangements involving one-party rule backed by the military. Also highly variegated are the views and policies of political and religious elites, especially with regard to capitalist market systems, projects of modernity, and processes of globalization. All such phenomena have important implications for practices and ideologies of gender and sexuality. In particular, they help explain the variation in Asia with respect to the tenor and degree of relative equality (or inequality) characteristic of male-female relations; women's status (in the sense of the prestige, honor, or esteem accorded them in relation to men); the ways in which femininity, masculinity, androgyny, intersexuality, and the like are understood, experienced, and represented; and the degree of legitimacy or stigma accorded to those who transgress one or another set of gendered or sexual norms.

In the pages that follow, I endeavor to convey a sense of the differences—as well as similarities—among Asian societies and cultures. In certain contexts, I also direct attention to some of the ways in which Asian societies and cultures both differ from and are similar to their counterparts in the West (and other world areas such as North Africa and Native North America). It is important to seek balance in any discussion of similarities and differences both within Asia and between Asia and the West. A focus only (or largely) on exoticized, "oriental" difference, for example, can easily understate the commonalities among Asian societies—or between Asia and the West. The problems are compounded when one engages in comparisons of the proverbial apples and oranges, as, for instance, when one compares Asian women's lived *experiences* with Western feminist *ideals* rather than comparing Asian and Western experiences or Asian and Western ideals, feminist or otherwise (Mohanty 1991).

Ritual, Religion, and Legitimating Ideologies

Asia's religious landscapes are rich and variegated, though underlying commonalities are readily apparent, especially in the ways religion bears on gender and sexuality. Buddhism, Confucianism, Christianity, Taoism, Islam, and Sikhism, for example, all of which are text-based religions with extensive scriptural traditions, are commonly viewed by scholars, as well as practitioners, as entailing various types of gender inequality (implicit, explicit, or both). This is partly because the most sacred figures in these traditions—for instance, Buddha, Confucius, Lao Tze, God and the prophet Jesus in the case of Christianity, and God and the prophet Muhammad in the case of Islam—are widely held to be unequivocally male. Many Hindu deities, by contrast are more ambiguously gendered. Siva, for example, the god of creation, destruction, and fertility, appears in some myths and religious art as entirely or largely male, in other contexts as essentially or predominantly female, and in yet other settings as ambiguously (or dual) gendered, sometimes experiencing gender, sexual, and other transformations of various kinds (e.g., from one to many and back again or vice versa).

Relevant as well is that for reasons explicated or conventionally seen as being signaled in scripture, males serve in each of these religious traditions as the main guardians and interpreters of sacred texts as well as the primary, if not sole, ritual practitioners, as also occurs in Judeo-Christian traditions. Females are commonly barred on scriptural grounds from the most sacred and prestigious ritual roles (although they often predominate in "peripheral cults" involving possession by spirits), many of which involve mediating between or otherwise linking humans and the realms of the sacred or the divine, and serving as exemplars or guides along the path(s) of moral and ethical righteousness. Similarly, females are more restricted than males in their access to sacred objects and locales (such as the Quran and the mosque and the inner sanctums of Hindu and Buddhist temples). The same is true for their involvement in more or less routine ritual practices (daily prayer, fasting, the gilding of "live" Buddha figures, etc.). This is partly because bodily processes and the exuviae and effluvia associated with menstruation and childbirth, though symbolizing a powerful capacity that men lack, tend to be seen by men and women alike as polluting, debilitating, or both.

As in Christianity and Judaism, masculinity and males are thus more closely linked in a symbolic sense with divinity, higher spiritual powers, and moral and ethical perfection than are femininity and females. These symbolic linkages have important implications for the ways in which differences between males and females are experienced, understood, and represented. They also inform relations between males and females.

These symbolic associations may legitimize gender inequalities that exist in households, families, economic domains, political arenas, and other venues of everyday life. This is not to suggest, however, that religions serve primarily to legitimize or rationalize inequalities. At least ideally, religions also provide intellectually and emotionally satisfying frameworks that enable believers to find or create meaning and order both in the routines of daily existence and in the potential challenges to meaning and order that are posed by illness, sickness, death, and other loss, as well as the hardships and injustices that people everywhere confront. By means of prescribed beliefs and attendant practices, many of which take place in collective or public settings, religions enable people to build communities ("churches") of the faithful and thus to transcend, if only temporarily, whatever existential isolation or material or other hardship or degradation they might experience. Providing mechanisms that allow for the overcoming of isolation and degradation and the building of community does not mean that all believers are treated equally. And, of course, by including some individuals or segments of a community within a religion or its inner sanctum, one is (by definition) simultaneously excluding others.

Some studies suggest that, all things being equal, female qualities and women as a whole tend to be accorded more prestige in societies that adhere to religious traditions in which female deities are prominent, as was the case in numerous "tribal" societies in Asia, Africa, and the Americas before the adoption of one or another world religion (Sanday 1981). It has also been suggested that, all things being equal, religious cosmologies such as Hinduism that prominently feature spirits and deities that are androgynous,

11

hermaphroditic, or dual gendered contribute to an atmosphere in which one or another degree of gender and sexual transgression is condoned, if not tacitly encouraged, at least for certain classes of individuals such as ritual specialists (shamans, seers, mediums, priests) and their partners (Roscoe 1996; Peletz 2006). This has long been the case in India in certain limited contexts. The castelike group of hermaphrodites and eunuchs known as *hijra*s, who dress and adorn themselves as women and are typically considered to be "neither man nor woman" (or "man plus woman") will be discussed later in this connection. Suffice it to note here that *hijra*s have long performed important rituals at weddings and the births of sons. They derive at least some of their legitimacy in popular culture from their explicit identification with Bahuchara Mata, "one of the many versions of the Mother Goddess worshipped throughout India," and with a strongly androgynous, if not bisexual, form of the "sexually ambivalent Siva" (Nanda 1993:373, 375).

In some societies in Asia, ritual specialists are not only allowed or expected to transgress gender and associated sexual expectations relevant to the majority of the population; they also help set the tone for the prevailing social ethos regarding gender and sexuality. This appears to have been the case for many areas of Southeast Asia since the beginning of early modern times (ca. 1500) (Peletz 2006, forthcoming). In many Southeast Asian societies, ritual specialists commonly engaged in transgender practices as well as same-sex relationships. While these practices and relations did not occur among all adults in the societies in question, they contributed to societywide atmospheres characterized by a good degree of pluralism with respect to gender and sexuality (as discussed below).

In light of the role of ritual specialists in Southeast Asia and elsewhere, a few words are in order concerning how rituals operate, especially in the relatively homogeneous, face-to-face communities that are home to many Asians. Rituals are sometimes formally defined as more or less invariant sequences of acts and/or utterances that are not usually encoded by the performer (Rappaport 1999). But this does not tell us much about the "work" of ritual. According to a leading scholar of ritual, it

> entails the establishment of convention, the sealing of social contract, the construction of the integrated conventional orders we . . . call Logoi (singular: Logos . . .), the investment of whatever it encodes with morality, . . . the representation of a paradigm of creation, the generation of the concept of the sacred and the sanctification of conventional order, the generation of theories of the occult, the evocation of numinous experience, the awareness of the divine, the grasp of the holy, and the construction of orders of meaning transcending the semantic (Rappaport 1999:27).

In sum, certain categories of rituals are of tremendous importance in establishing moral order, paradigms of creation, notions of the sacred, and so on; their gendered meanings are likewise of deep significance.

Exploring Gender Ideologies (Malay Muslims, Burmese Buddhists, and North Indian Hindus)

Gender ideologies are usually very complex, with profound implications for the ways women and men view their worlds and experience the terms in which they live their lives. A consideration of gendered symbols and idioms among Malay Muslims, the dominant ethnic group in multiethnic, multireligious Malaysia, will illustrate the internal logic of gender ideologies, how they legitimize male privilege, and some of the ways in which elements of these ideologies are reworked in everyday life to challenge hierarchies of gender. I conclude with a brief overview of gender ideologies among Burmese Buddhists and North Indian Hindus, which reveals some of the underlying similarities in seemingly disparate ideologies of gender.

One important caveat is that most of my comments on Malay Muslims focus on rural Malays in the state of Negeri Sembilan. The Malays in this state have much in common with Malays residing elsewhere in the Malay Peninsula (West Malaysia) in terms of language, religion, and gender (e.g., all Malays speak the Malay language and are Muslims), but they also differ from them in certain ways. Most relevant is that their social organization is usually characterized as matrilineal in that it includes clans and lineages of matrilineal design in which descent and inheritance are traced through the female line. This reflects the Minangkabau (West Sumatran) ancestry of the area's earliest permanent settlers. Malays elsewhere in the peninsula tend to lack clans and lineages as well as systems of descent and inheritance emphasizing ties through women. As with most other Southeast Asians and most Americans of European background, their social structures are usually referred to as bilateral (or cognatic).

I begin with an explication of *nafsu*, an Arabic-origin term (*nafs* in Arabic) that is widely used among Malays, most other Muslims in the Malay-Indonesian archipelago (e.g., Acehnese, Minangkabau, and Javanese), and Muslims worldwide. It is translated in contemporary Malay dictionaries as "passion," "desire," "lust," "want," "longing," and so forth, which is in keeping with its uses both in the field site of Bogang and in other Muslim communities.[1] In many Muslim communities, the term *nafsu* (hereafter "passion") frequently carries derogatory connotations, especially when it is applied to humans. In many Muslim communities, moreover, one finds an entrenched, highly elaborated belief that passion is more pronounced among women than men. The latter point will be addressed below. First, however, we need to contextualize such beliefs by examining Bogang villagers' general understandings of passion and the ways they relate to local understandings and representations of "reason" (*akal*). As will be apparent in due course, passion and reason are not simply symbols "of" or "about" gender. They also inform village thought about the essence and dynamics of human nature, social relations, and the world at large, all of which is to say that they are central to the local ontology.

In the Malay view of things, God created the universe with all of its features and inhabitants. In accordance with God's will, passion is present in humans and other animals, spirits, and other living creatures. The presence of passion in humans, and in the universe generally, dates from the time of Adam, who, after seeing two doves, asked God to make him a companion or mate. God obliged Adam and made Hawah (Eve) from one of Adam's ribs. God proceeded to instruct Adam and Hawah not to eat the fruit of a certain tree (a pomegranate tree in some local variants of the myth, an unspecified tree in others). But Adam and Hawah were tempted by the devil to eat the fruit. When they did so, they were driven from heaven. A piece of the fruit lodged in Adam's throat, and to this day men have "Adam's apples," which serve as embodied reminders of Adam's transgression. Portions of the apple appeared as breasts in Hawah, and to this day women have prominent breasts, which, like men's Adam's apples, signify both Adam and Hawah's sins and humankind's passion.

The moral of this myth of genesis is not only that those who disobey God receive divine punishment, but also—and more relevant here—that sensual and other kinds of gratification necessarily entail both the indulgence of desire and the absence of restraint. Restraint and control of the inner self are strongly marked moral virtues, the attainment of which brings prestige. Conversely, the absence of restraint signifies a lack of virtue and brings stigma.

This system of moral evaluation helps explain Malay villagers' marked ambivalence about the satisfaction of basic (biophysiological) human requirements. On the one hand, villagers recognize that human beings require food, drink, air, shelter, and the like, if they are to survive and thrive. And they are well aware that sexual activity is necessary for procreation and the reproduction of society and culture. On the other hand, villagers view the satisfaction of these basic human requirements with marked ambivalence since their satisfaction is associated with the absence of restraint. People look down on individuals who are overly concerned with food, eating, and drinking, even though this is one of two domains in which relative indulgence is permitted, even enjoined (the other is illness, real or imagined). And they talk about such behavior in terms of the preponderance, if only temporary, of passion relative to reason, which is seen as unsightly, unbecoming, morally offensive, and, at least in some contexts, seriously sinful. More generally, when villagers speak of gossiping, desiring material possessions, or being especially (or overly) interested in sex, they often mention passion; they are, moreover, quick to link passion with the devil and evil spirits and demons of various kinds who tempt them with sinful behavior.

Negative attitudes toward the absence of restraint are illustrated in villagers' views concerning food prohibitions and ethnic groups that appear not to observe any such prohibitions such as the seminomadic non-Muslim aborigines living in the hilly, forested regions behind the village. The aborigines eat the meat of wild boar, which, like all pork, is forbidden to Muslims and is highest on the list of prohibited foods as far as Malays are concerned. The consumption of pork is seen by Malays as thoroughly revolting, far more so than the consumption of snake, dog, and lizard, which the aborigines are also said to enjoy. Because the aborigines eat wild boar, Malays assume they do not have any food prohibitions. And because they have no food prohibitions they "have no religion, only beliefs and superstitions."

More broadly, since the aborigines have no religion they have no culture, which, in the local view, is what distinguishes human beings from "mere animals." The idea that the aborigines exercise no restraint when it comes to eating pork and are for this reason uncultured and subhuman resonates both with villagers' negative views of other "races" (Chinese, Indians, and "white people" [*orang putih*]) whose behavior—especially with respect to eating, drinking, gambling, and sex—is seen as relatively unrestrained, and with their views of fellow Malays whose behavior is deemed inappropriate or aesthetically offensive. The exercise (or absence) of restraint thus serves as an important ethnic marker as well as an index of virtue (or its absence) within Malay communities. In cases of seriously offensive behavior, Malays sometimes say that the offending individual is *kurang ajar*, a literal translation of which is "less than fully taught"—a very serious charge.

Persons whose comportment is offensive are thus said to be improperly socialized and therefore standing somewhere between the rule-governed realm of humans, where socialization entails the learning and internalization of moral codes, and the world of animals, which is governed by passion, not by moral codes or rules. Socialization is seen as a process involving the gradual curtailment or control of passion through the imposition of "man-made" (but ultimately divinely inspired) codes and rules embodied in Islam and *adat* (tradition, custom, customary law). The socialization process, and culture generally, thus "works on" the raw material of passion, which is directly and inextricably associated with the world of animals and nature and with the relatively, if not altogether, uncultured (natural) behavior of other "races."

The other key symbol invoked by Malays when they discuss similarities and differences among males and females is *akal*, an Arabic-origin concept (*'aql* in Arabic) that is of central importance among Muslims throughout Southeast Asia and beyond. The term denotes "reason," "intelligence," and "rationality," the ability to evaluate alternative courses of action (e.g., to display perspective and view things from afar) and render informed judgments, and is widely used in Malay culture in connection with passion (and "shame" [*malu*]). As mentioned earlier, it is often said that *akal* (hereafter "reason") distinguishes humans from the rest of the animal world and is a special gift from God. Reason "cooperates" or "works together" with both the liver (the seat of emotions) and *iman* (faith, strong belief or trust in God, resoluteness, sincerity) to guide the individual along the proper path(s). Villagers also contend that reason and passion forever struggle against one another within the individual and that "good behavior" is evidence of the preponderance, however temporary or qualified, of reason over passion, just as "bad behavior" reflects the dominance, however short-lived or partial, of passion over reason. Shame is relevant here as well, for it, too, acts as a brake on passion and its expression in social action.

While (normal, healthy) human beings are born with the capacity to develop reason, they do not display or possess reason at birth. Rather, in the normal course of things, reason "develops" or "expands" over time, as a consequence of socialization and religious instruction in particular, and is typically manifested in one or another form when a child is seven to eight years old or, as some people put it, when the child begins instruction in the recitation of the Quran (at the age of six or seven).

Diligent observance of Muslim prayer procedures and other religious strictures is one way to develop one's reason. Conversely, the cultivation of reason through concentration and various types of mental and spiritual exercises entailing studied restraint facilitates proper prayer and other forms of religiously valued and morally virtuous behavior. Compared to children and adolescents, adults tend to have more extensive obligations as Muslims and to take them more seriously. This is one reason why adults are typically regarded as having more reason than children and adolescents. Others include their superior abilities (relative to children and adolescents) to make informed judgments based on experience in the world; their demonstrated capacities to perform the tasks associated with domestic maintenance, production, and the like; their greater control over their passion; and their more systematic internalization of and behavioral adherence to the moral norms of Malay culture, hence (given the explicit link between being Malay and being human) their stronger commitment to being human.

While the acquisition or development of reason is a gradual process, so, too, in many cases is the dissolution or loss of reason in the course of debilitating illness or old age. Individuals afflicted with senility are often said to have lost their reason and to have reverted to a childlike state in which reason is poorly developed or only sporadically manifest. In some instances, senescence seems to be regarded as a natural process that is inherent in biological aging, though in others it is attributed to possession by evil spirits harbored by malevolent (human) others.

Various types of severe emotional, psychological, and spiritual disorders (including senility) are sometimes attributed to or regarded as entailing debilitated reason, but for the most part disorders of this sort are conceptualized in terms of livers and/or "life forces" (*semangat*). Thus, a person who exhibits what we might take to be symptoms of extreme anxiety, depression, or obsessive behavior is not usually viewed as having something wrong with his or her reason or brain but rather to be suffering from an affliction of the liver or life force. (Mental retardation and insanity, on the other hand, are seen as disorders of the brain, mind, or reason.) It is nonetheless true that disturbances of the liver or life force can interfere with one's ability to reason. In this sense, Malays view body and mind as integrally related parts of a single and unified whole and do not operate with a dualistic mind-body dichotomy of the sort that informs Western medicine and Western thought as a whole.

I have already remarked that Malays frequently contend that passion and reason are present to one degree or another in all humans but that passion is present in greater concentrations or more pronounced among women, whereas reason is less so. These latter contentions, which are part of Malays' "official" discourse on gender and are clearly hegemonic in Raymond Williams's (1977) sense of the term, focus on the culturally elaborated perception that women are less controlled and restrained than men, insofar as they are more prone to gossiping and desiring material possessions, and are otherwise more closely tied to the "baser" things in life. The arena of sexual relations is the quintessential context, at least (or especially) for men, through which women's stronger passion is displayed; for, as some male elders told me, women "still want more" even after their husbands are thoroughly satisfied (have achieved orgasm). This particular contention, which may well derive in part from men's (and women's) limited understandings of the anatomy and physiology of female orgasm, was never conceded by women (more precisely, it never came up) in the numerous conversations that I or my wife had with them. Nor was the point made by another male elder that "women in hotels" (a reference to prostitutes) can have sex "ten or twenty times in an evening or even all night long," none of which would be possible for a man. I should emphasize, though, that many women *do* espouse the position that women's passion is more pronounced than men's. Moreover, virtually all women hold that they "need to"—and do in fact—have a stronger sense of "shame" (*malu*) than men since, if they did not, they would be "like wild animals" and chaos would reign in the world.

Malay views of the sort outlined here appear to be of great antiquity. In light of the Arabic origin of the concepts of reason and passion and the centrality of these concepts in Islamic discourse, it seems reasonable to assume that such views were introduced into the Malay Peninsula along with Islam, beginning around the thirteenth century, and that, due to the subsequent historical development of Islam in the region, they became increasingly prevalent in the centuries that followed. Significantly, the gendered differences encoded in these views not only provided much of the cultural rationale for restricting elite women's involvement in formal political arenas in Muslim communities in Southeast Asia during the latter part of the period 1450–1800; they also served to delegitimize commoner women's important roles in public communal rituals during this time, thus effecting both a constriction and an overall devaluation of women's ritual activities (Reid 1988, 1993; B. Andaya 1994, 2000; Peletz 2006, forthcoming). Gender-skewed political and ritual institutions, in turn, have fostered the reproduction of all such views associated with official representations of gender. So, too, have myriad components of civil society, including official kinship (which represents marriage and affinal exchange in terms of men exchanging women) and various Islamic institutions such as mosques and religious courts. Also relevant are spirit possession and *latah* (a cultural elaboration of the startle reflex), both of which predominate among women and are interpreted by women and men alike as evidence of women's greater "animality" and spiritual weakness vis-à-vis those of men (Peletz 1996).

These (official) views of the differences between men and women are congruent with the (official) gender imagery found among Malays elsewhere in the peninsula; among Acehnese, Javanese, and other Muslims in Southeast Asia; and among Muslims in other parts of the Islamic world (though there are some striking contrasts as well).[2] One comprehensive account of such imagery comes from Morocco and indicates not only that there is an important developmental dynamic that needs to be considered when assessing Moroccan views of males and females (such views change over the life cycle) but also that, in what might be termed private or "backstage" contexts, some Moroccan women contest official representations concerning both their secondary status and the differences between males and females generally (Dwyer 1978). These findings are relevant to Negeri Sembilan as well. In some ways far more interesting, however, is the manner in which gender imagery in Negeri Sembilan differs from what has been reported for Morocco, other North African groups such as Egyptian Bedouins (Abu-Lughod 1986), and most other societies, including Malays outside of Negeri Sembilan. To wit:

in Negeri Sembilan there is a highly elaborated alternative discourse, which is in many respects an inversion of the official discourse that I have outlined here and clearly transcends private, domestic, or female-dominated contexts. In short, key features of this very public discourse are espoused by men and women alike.

The alternative discourse to which I refer is composed of "practical" representations of gender. In contrast to their official counterparts, these representations are not "explicitly codified in . . . quasi-juridical formalism" (Bourdieu 1977:35). Compared with official representations, moreover, they are more thoroughly grounded in the everyday practical situations in which people find themselves. An additional point of contrast is that, while they, too, have legitimizing functions, they are more explicitly oriented to practical realities such as managing money and other household resources, taking care of children and other relatives (including the elderly and infirm), maintaining exchange relationships with neighboring households and the members of one's lineage and clan, and in these and other ways ensuring domestic reproduction. Finally, whereas some practical representations simply differ from, or are largely irrelevant to, official representations, others constitute subversive challenges to them and are in this sense appropriately characterized as counterhegemonic.

Practical representations of gender portray men as less reasonable (i.e., having less reason) and less responsible than women both with regard to managing money and other household resources and in terms of honoring basic social obligations associated with marriage, parenting, and kinship generally. They also depict men as less deserving (and in need) of subsistence guarantees than women, a point to which I will return in a moment. These representations both derive from and inform the ways in which people experience, understand, and represent kinship (particularly marriage and divorce), reciprocity, and social reproduction. And, not surprisingly, they permeate everyday discourse concerning the gendered nature of property and inheritance relations, especially why it is that daughters continue to be favored over sons in the inheritance of houses and land, even when the latter are not formally classified as "ancestral"—hence exclusively female—property.

Daughters continue to be favored over sons in the inheritance of houses and land partly because women are believed to require greater subsistence guarantees than men insofar as they are held to be less flexible, resourceful, and adaptive than men, who, it is believed, can eke out a living wherever they find themselves. It is also taken for granted that all women will marry and have children and that they must have resources to fall back on, particularly since they may not always be able to depend on their husbands. The latter may be involved in temporary outmigration for many months or years at a stretch, or may simply predecease their wives. Of greater cultural salience is the issue of desertion and divorce by husbands. Marriage is regarded as a tenuous arrangement (two-thirds of all marriages in Bogang end in divorce),[3] for men's commitments to their wives and children are seen as provisional, even capricious. In the final analysis, then, women merit greater subsistence guarantees than men not only, or even primarily, because they are held to be the less flexible, resourceful, and adaptive of the two sexes but because they must be protected from men, most notably their husbands but also their brothers and men in other kinship and social roles.

Thus, these practical representations of gender portray men as less reliable and trustworthy than women and relatively uncommitted to their wives, children, and other relatives. They also depict men as fond of gambling (and alcohol),[4] overly inclined to purchase on credit, prone to running up burdensome debts, and thus less restrained—and in certain respects more impassioned—than women. In the practical view, moreover, men are "at fault" in most cases of divorce since, as some of my male informants put it, "they don't follow the rules," are "basically lazy," and "expect to eat for free."

As a comparison with this overview of the ways in which Malay Muslims understand and represent similarities and differences among males and females,[5] I want to consider briefly gender ideologies among Burmese Buddhists. These ideologies have much in common with those of Theravada Buddhists in Thailand and Cambodia (Kirsch 1982, 1985; Keyes 1984; Van Esterik 2000; Ledgerwood 1994; Smith-Hefner 1999) and are in some respects strikingly similar to those of Malay Muslims, though they are cast in different symbols and idioms and pressed into service in somewhat different ways.

Melford Spiro (1997) has summarized a range of Burmese Buddhist beliefs bearing on gender in relation to two ideological complexes, "the ideology of the superior male" and "the ideology of the dangerous female." The first of these complexes posits that males are superior to females

> because of their sexual anatomy and *hpoun*. The Burmese regard the penis as a "noble" organ, a "golden flower," and the vagina as "ignoble" and polluting. *Hpoun*, an ineffable psychospiritual essence that is possessed only by males (and a famous female disciple of the Buddha) is usually translated as "glory" but is perhaps more accurately glossed as "charisma" . . . Since males alone are born with *hpoun*, they are innately higher than females intellectually, morally, and spiritually. (20–21)

Spiro (21, 22) goes on to explain that, according to Burmese views, "the moral superiority of males is evinced by the alleged prevalence among females of three moral defects": greed, lust—a "woman's sexual passion is [held to be] eight times stronger than a man's"—and assorted evil practices that include "habitually visiting others, making their husbands angry, [and] neglecting domestic duties." More generally, "the spiritual superiority of males is attested to by their special place in Buddhist teaching and practice. The Buddhist initiation ceremony (*hsimbyu*) and induction into the Buddhist monastic order (*sangha*) are both restricted to males. Moreover, rebirth as a male is a sine qua non for the attainment of the three highest levels of spiritual achievement— sainthood, Buddhahood, and nirvana" (22).

The second complex ("the ideology of the dangerous female"), for its part, postulates the existence of female dangers to men that are simultaneously moral, emotional, and sexual. These dangers include mercurial emotions, treachery, "love magic," "an extraordinarily powerful libido, a polluting vagina, and sexual allure" (Spiro 1997:25), any of which can threaten male authority and control along with the *hpoun* associated with it.

Spiro demonstrates that Burmese women, whether living in villages, urban areas, or diasporic communities in the West, tend to internalize and reproduce key features of these beliefs in much the same way and to the same general degree as Burmese men, even while they question and subvert others (see, e.g., Belak 2002; and Skidmore 2004).[6] My research among Malay Muslims has led me to similar conclusions, though I want to underscore that neither Spiro nor I—nor the many other researchers who have encountered similar dynamics in their field sites—are engaged in "blaming the victim". We are simply pointing out that gender ideologies, which begin to be internalized, largely unconsciously, during infancy, and are usually implicit rather than explicit, are extremely powerful, pervasive, and all-encompassing—partly because sanctified by religion—all the more so because they are often both conveyed and internalized as basic common sense. It should be noted in any case that the extent to which women or members of any other social group internalize dominant ideologies—or construct alternative ideologies that may challenge hegemonic discourses—is an empirical question that must be addressed in each context.

Perspectives from Hindu communities in India are of interest in this connection. Hindu ideologies of gender share general features of Muslim and Buddhist gender ideologies—they devalue women, for example, and rationalize this devaluation in terms of women's supposed anatomical, physiological, and spiritual deficiencies—even while they are quite distinct from Muslim and Buddhist ideologies as regards the specific symbols, idioms, and metaphors in which they are cast. Particularly relevant is the fact that Hindu cultural traditions depict women in morally contradictory terms. They accord great value to women's fertility and its positive implications for the biological and social reproduction of households, patrilineal kin groups, village, nation, and religion, but they simultaneously portray female sexuality as volatile, dangerous, and potentially destructive of hearth, home, and more encompassing moral communities.

In their studies of women's oral traditions in the states of Rajasthan and Uttar Pradesh in northern India, the anthropologists Gloria Raheja and Ann Gold (1994) found that village women, even when veiled and otherwise appearing to behave in accordance with the patriarchal conventions of local kinship and gender, exercise a good deal of agency and commonly protest the discrimination, verbal abuse, and suffering they experience at the hands of male kin and mothers-in-law. They also actively contest many features of Hindu religious doctrines that devalue or denigrate them, encourage them to be embarrassed and ashamed about their bodies and sexualities, and trivialize their yearnings, loves, and losses, though here, too, the ways they do so vary by region and class. Based on their extensive study of women's ordinary conversations and autobiographical accounts, and on their highly nuanced and incisive analyses of the ditties and songs (some of which are hilariously obscene) that women recite at births, at weddings, and on festival days, the anthropologists reject Stanley Tambiah's (1989:418) suggestion that the critiques and other challenges contained in North Indian women's songs and other narrative genres might be "context-restricted 'rituals of rebellion' that leave the dominant male ideology more or less intact" (cited in Raheja and Gold 1994:24). They argue instead that "the songs and stories may enter . . . [women's] lives and shift, however slightly or however consequentially, the terms in which their lives are led" (26; see also Gold 2002). In this context, then, as in many others in India, "everyday forms of resistance" (Scott 1985) that occur within the walls of the household or outside its boundaries may be deeply meaningful, even though they do not involve the large-scale, organized, collective, overt forms of protest that Western observers often take to be diagnostic of dissent. The same may be said of Malaysia, Burma, and other Asian settings.

Households, Factory Daughters, and the Cultural Politics of Weddings (Japan and Korea)

Throughout Asia, as in the rest of the world, the household is the origin and locus of an individual's most valued and enduring personal relationships, public identity, and emotional mooring. The interior of a house, moreover, and to a lesser extent the surrounding yard (if there is one), is often viewed as the relatively private and somewhat exclusive domain of the individuals living there. In theory, what transpires within the confines of a house or among its members should not concern persons of other households; at the risk of overstating the case, it is "none of their business." In practice, however, the concept of a private or domestic realm refers more to the relative social autonomy of individuals in their own homes and to the fact that adult members of a household are not usually (or necessarily) beholden to anyone else so long as they appear to uphold basic community norms. But there is a catch here and a problem for villagers and urban residents alike: much of what goes on in the domestic domain is eminently public in that it can be heard and seen by immediate neighbors, passersby, and others. In some cases, moreover, such as the Malay village in which I conducted much of my fieldwork in the 1970s and 1980s, most houses rest on ancestral land over which sisters and their matrilineally related kin hold residual rights. This fact bears significantly on the married males of these households—who are typically born and raised in other communities and are usually strangers to one another prior to their marriages to women of the same residential compound or village—and on the status of in-marrying males overall. In short, notions of privacy and the private or domestic domain are culturally distinctive and highly variable.

A focus on the households in which people live and how the members of households both cooperate and at times struggle with one another in their efforts to meet their (individual and collective) material, social, and emotional needs provides grounded perspectives on gender and sexuality that complement, complicate, and in many cases qualify the picture(s) we receive from religious doctrines alone. In rural areas especially, households are typically units of consumption and ritual activity, as well as units of production, and, as noted earlier, loci of moral anchorage and a key source of their residents' emotional support and social identity. In virtually all societies, the proper and smooth functioning of households is seen as requiring not only a division of labor by gender and generation, a division that serves to unite household residents via interdependence as much as—if not more than—it actually "divides," but also the sharing, pooling, and "patchworking" of resources (to borrow a term from Nazli Kibria's [1993] study of Vietnamese in the diaspora). Notions of filial duty, much valorized in the religious traditions of Confucianism, Buddhism, and Islam, are relevant here because they are commonly invoked to mobilize the loyalties, labor power, and other resources of children in the ostensible interests ("survival strategy," reproduction) of the household and, in some cases, those of the lineage and clan as a whole. Doctrines of filial piety along with comportment attuned to them may thus be a source of great comfort and solace to elders but they can also be experienced as stressful, repressive, or both by those who are enjoined to honor their parents' (and grandparents') wishes and unspoken expectations. In her studies of factory women in rapidly industrializing Java, Diane Wolf (1990, 1992) examines both sides of this coin. In the process she debunks, the myth of the "oriental" household "that runs smoothly under the rational guidance of a [stern and] solitary patriarch"

(Kendall 1996:161), noting, among other things, that female factory workers in Java, like wage-earning women in many other parts of Asia, commonly deploy behavioral strategies geared toward circumventing the multiple inequities entailed in households structured by kinship (which encodes gender and generation) and systems of capitalist production. Wolf acknowledges that younger household members often make sacrifices for their elders and others. But as one reviewer put it she also "faults the 'domestic strategy model' for masking profound inequalities within families under the rubric of a 'common good,' for blinding researchers to generational and gendered conflict within domestic groups, and above all, for ignoring the significance of agency where individual family members 'may engage in behaviors that are passive, non-strategic, overtly resistant, antagonistic, ambivalent, antistrategic, or even multistrategic'" (161).[7]

In Japan, as elsewhere, individuals' households continue to be of widely ramifying emotional and economic significance, though the experience and meaning of living in a household varies by generation, gender, and class. The Japanese household, traditionally known as the *ie*, is "designated by a character which can mean the physical building of the house or the household line . . . ; [e]tymologically it carries the meaning of 'hearth,' signifying people who belonged to the same descent group" (Kondo 1990:121). There has long been considerable variation in the actual organization and operation of the Japanese household. One reason for this is that the household is vested with economic and socioreligious functions whose fulfillment may take precedence over all else, leading some to characterize the household as a "task performance unit" (Pelzel 1970, cited in Kondo 1990:122). Another, related reason is that "biological kinship counts for relatively little in Japan, when compared with the importance of 'blood' in, for example, Chinese, Korean, or American kinship" (162). According to traditional ideals

> the *ie* is patriarchal, patrilineal, primogenitural, and patrilocal. Succession to the headship of the household is reserved, ideally, for the eldest son, who inherits the household property as part of the process of succession [unless he is deemed incompetent, in which case a son-in-law or another male may be groomed for the role]. The eldest son also [ideally] inherits the responsibility of caring for his aged parents, with whom he resides. Younger sons establish branch families with the aid of the main family. Financial aid given to younger sons to support their efforts at branching is likened to the dowries that daughters take with them when they marry out: both are forms of premortem inheritance. A marriage, preferably arranged, has more to do with the interests of the *ie* as a whole than with those of the man and woman as individuals. In terms of intrahousehold status, the system calls for a ranking of the

aged over the young, elder sons over younger, sons over daughters, males over females. (Hamabata 1990:33–34).

The reproduction of the household line is of great concern, as are the potentially expansive networks of kinship created through the marital and affinal ties that link households with one another. These concerns are felt most strongly by parents and grandparents, and by those situated at or near the top of the status hierarchy, for they often have "more property, more responsibility, perhaps more tradition, at stake" (Kondo 1990:316 n. 10). Concerns of the latter sort help explain not only why parents, especially in the middle and upper classes, still feel strongly committed to arranging marriages for their children but also why middle- and upper-class children continue to be receptive to arranged marriages or at least arranged dating with the potential for marriage. Women in these classes are subject to greater pressure to accept marriages arranged for them by female kin and go-betweens just as they are apparently more likely to internalize duty as desire or at least to harmonize duty and desire in ways that recognize "that romantic love, *ren'ai,* cannot be counted on, cannot be the foundation on which to build one's life. What lasts, what supports, what becomes the basis of security is the household" (Hamabata 1990:135).

Anthropologist Matthews Hamabata (1990:162) has written that "From a distance, the [Japanese] household seems populated with automatons, whose discharge of duties proceeds along lines both dispassionate and rational. The household seems, in fact, machine efficient and machine cold." Based on his extensive fieldwork among elite business families, however, Hamabata found that households in Japan are "nearly bursting with vengeance, passionate love, anger, ambition, nurturing care, envy, all of the exalted and sullied aspects of human nature and human emotion . . . The individual's desire to influence the course of his or her own destiny, the need to love and be loved, sometimes desperate, are given form by, and, in turn, shape, the culture and social structure of the *ie.*"

Researchers throughout the world have underscored that the gendered division of labor within the household informs women's and men's activities and relationships beyond the household as well. Gender ideologies in most societies in Asia, as elsewhere, assign women a greater share of domestic responsibility related to cooking, cleaning, the rearing of infants and children, and the overall maintenance and reproduction of the household as a meaningful social unit. In imperial Japan (1900–1945), state-sanctioned ideologies celebrating the "good wife and wise mother" (*ryosai kenbo*) codified the ideal roles of women, which were held to flow from their very "nature." Ideologies such as these, which drew on Confucian ideals and "cults of domesticity" that developed in the West in the nineteenth century (Tamanoi 1990:26), influence how women and men are situated in the paid labor force and in relation to military and other public services, important contexts for displaying heroism and patriotism and thus garnering prestige. More broadly, these ideologies help position women and men vis-à-vis both the state—which in the mid-twentieth century granted women the right to vote, bring lawsuits, and petition for divorce—and public domains generally.

Domestic responsibilities assigned to women, in accordance with gender ideologies bearing on women's "natural essences" and appropriate and inappropriate female spheres, often preclude their full-time participation in the paid labor force (as factory or construction workers, artisans, or professionals of another kind) and thus influence not only their earning power and relative social and economic autonomy in relation to their husbands but also their public identity and sense of self. So, too, do culturally inseparable ideologies bearing on masculinity and the public sphere that grant women access to masculinized public domains only under certain conditions and only in certain sexualized or moral roles: the prostitute, the geisha, "the café waitress and the modern girl, or the puritanical reformist who challenge[s] masculine sexual behaviour, censure[s] the modern girls, or attempt[s] to clean up the political system" (Mackie 2003:64). Noteworthy exceptions such as these aside, Japanese women are still largely unable to "enter public space without arousing [male] anxiety about their presence" (ibid.; see also Robertson 1998:14–15 passim).

Much of the Western scholarship produced in the 1970s and 1980s on management styles and relationships among workers in Japanese factories and other business enterprises focused on men (especially salarymen [*sarariman*]). This scholarship commonly obscured the fact that while "Japanese women participate in the labor force at rates similar to those among women in Western societies, . . . the nature of that participation differs significantly from that in other industrialized nations" (Tamanoi 1990:25). As the anthropologist Mariko Tamanoi describes the situation, "[Japanese] women remain poorly paid; few single women working in large corporations can climb the career ladder; there is little or no job training for women; most married women work in medium- or small-scale enterprises, and many work in so called part-time jobs that are in fact full-time or over-time; most women are not unionized, and unions do not necessarily support workers" (25). These generalizations receive support from Dorinne Kondo's incisive study of Japanese women employed in small family-owned factories in the Arakawa ward of Tokyo. Kondo found that in order to be considered a "real artisan" (the factory produced upscale bakery goods) one must work "full time," at least twelve hours per day (and much longer during periods of peak demand), and that definitions of "real artisanship" thus exclude virtually all women since the close to eight hours a day they typically put in is construed by management and seasoned full-timers alike as "part time" (1990:252, 289–90 passim). Business enterprises (much like schools and other institutions) continue the work begun in households and families of socializing individuals through strict timetables and other regulatory schemes that inculcate certain types of habits, dispositions, and sentiments in their subjects and otherwise discipline bodies, minds, and souls alike (cf. Ong 1987). Hence, full-timers, who are almost always male, are multiply privileged. Put differently, because "a mature artisan is a man who, in crafting fine objects, crafts a finer self," women are seen as crafting neither fine objects nor fine selves (Kondo 1990:241).

That said, the factory women Kondo came to know fashion meaningful identities and senses of self. They manage to do so partly by drawing on their gendered experiences in the power-laden social fields constituting families, households, and companies that represent themselves as families and partly through self-cultivation via calligraphy, flower arranging, archery, painting, poetry, and so on. Japanese factory women are not the docile, subservient, "unidimensional . . . automaton-like workers happily singing the company song, burning with enthusiasm for their quality control circles" that they are often assumed to be in the public imaginations of Japanese and westerners alike (1990:301, 315 n. 8).

Whether or not they work in factories, as increasing numbers of them do, the vast majority of young Japanese and other Asians plan on getting married. If the recent past and the present are any indication of future trends, the manner in which spouses are chosen and weddings celebrated will continue to be fraught with conflicting desires and expectations. This should not be surprising since parents (along with grandparents and other relatives) often have a great deal invested in their children's marital choices, wedding ceremonies, and postmarital affinal relations, and they tend to view all such matters from across an increasingly gaping generational divide. What is typically at stake is not only how parents and others who sponsor or host weddings (or are otherwise implicated in them by virtue of kin ties to one of the spouses) choose or are able to represent themselves—their virtues and honor, which are often tied to the reputations of their female kin, and their material standing—to the community. Also at stake is their ability to ensure the household's future viability and in some cases (such as rural China and rural Vietnam) the continuity of lineage and clan. In Muslim contexts (Malaysia, Indonesia, and Pakistan, for example) and elsewhere, a woman's bridal attire may emerge as a site of contestation, as when one group of relatives seeks a modest or "traditional" outfit and another group of kin or the bride herself opts for something more "modern" or "cosmopolitan."

Here, as elsewhere, notions of what is traditional, cosmopolitan, and modern are by no means self-evident. In Muslim Southeast Asia (Indonesia, Malaysia, Brunei, southern Thailand, and the southern Philippines), for instance, women did not usually don veils or other self-consciously Islamic headgear prior to the Islamic resurgence that began, in mostly urban areas, in the 1970s and 1980s. For some such women, headgear and wedding attire construed as Islamic are defined in opposition to more traditional (read "insufficiently Islamic") garb and are clear gestures of affinity with the modern Islamic world. In these and other Asian settings, potential conflicts over the symbols and meanings of bridal attire are sometimes ameliorated, though they can also be exacerbated, by newly created "wedding traditions" whereby the bride dons "traditional" attire for one part of the wedding and wears a modern, Western-style wedding gown (complete with a gauzy lace veil and a long train) for another.

The Korean case is instructive here and is in some ways similar to what one finds in Taiwan, Japan, and Singapore.[8] In these countries, Christianity is emblematic of modernity for increasing segments of the population (even though most people identify as Confucian and/or Buddhist) and having a "Christian wedding" is for a variety of reasons a key symbol of being modern or cosmopolitan, as opposed to "old fashioned," "backward," "provincial," "heathen," or worse. This is also true in the overwhelmingly Catholic Philippines, even among some minorities in highland areas and some Muslims communities in the southern regions of the country. More generally, as the anthropologist Laurel Kendall (1996:ix) writes in *Getting Married in Korea*, weddings are "flash points of argument about the past and the present, about the desirability of women and men, and about what it means to be Korean in a shifting and intensely commodified milieu." Heated public debates center on many facets of marriage, each in its own way a barometer of the health and well-being of the social body, from the dilemmas of aging bachelors in rural settings subject to massive out-migration who have increasingly dim prospects of obtaining a wife and thus attaining social adulthood to "the high cost of dowries exacted from working women, the extortionate fees charged by professional matchmakers who pander to the very rich, the superficiality, expense, and excessively 'Western' flavor of contemporary ceremonies, and the deeply rooted patriarchal premises of all Korean marriage custom" (15). As in Japan, debates in Korea over "matchmade" (*chungmae*) versus "love" (*yonae*) marriages are simultaneously debates "about the past and the future, about morality, about identity, and about the lives of women and men as they have moved through . . . [the] twentieth century" and into the new millennium (3).

The "new style" (*sinsik*) weddings that were all the rage in Korea in the 1970s and 1980s owe much to Christian missionaries who sought to convert "heathen" (Confucian) Koreans to the path of God beginning in the late nineteenth century. Missionaries introduced white wedding gowns and white lace veils in hopes of replacing "the woman in antique dress, her face veiled behind her long sleeves, only half seen and all unseeing, her eyelids glued shut with rice paste" (Kendall 1996:64, 93). This change occurred in China as well in the context of more encompassing Chinese efforts to reform wedding rites and the institutions of marriage and family, a goal that simultaneously involved reducing women's subservient position in society at large—attacking traditional womanhood as "one of the hallmarks of traditional culture and a symbol of national weakness" (Sang 2003:43). As in China, nationalist reformers in Korea, including students and intellectuals, embraced some of these goals, influenced as they were by Enlightenment ideals disseminated by missionaries and other Westerners as well as humiliation stemming from Korea's colonization by Japan (1910–45). Reformers thus questioned a broad range of Confucian strictures emphasizing, among other things, filial piety (*hyo*). These included the sanctified expectations that sons will engage in ritual and other practices venerating their fathers, grandfathers, and more distant ancestral figures and the formal barring of daughters from all such ritual activity (and thus from accruing the moral virtue resulting therefrom). Also subject to questioning and declining legitimacy were a broad range of "superstitious" ceremonies associated with birth, death, and the agricultural cycle that involved predominantly female shamans, as well as a whole series of kinship practices. The latter included various customs associated with patrilineal descent; the favoring in inheritance of firstborn sons and males generally (daughters tended to be excluded from inheritance); and postmarital residence involving patrilocality, which typically entailed a bride moving in with (and to one or another degree being incorporated into) her husband's family and kin group and effectively severing ties with her natal kin and the more encompassing kin group into which she was born.

Some of the specifics of the new-style weddings merit brief comment. The *churye*, who is in charge of the ceremonies, "merge[s] the role of the virtuous elder who officiated at Confucian rites with the image of the Christian minister; his role also recalls that of the *tanomare nakodo* who presides at Japanese weddings, another prototype [dating from the colonial period] . . . available to those who participated in the construction of the new wedding" (Kendall 1998:65, n. 17). More broadly, the new wedding "celebrates conjugality in symbolic counterpoint to the old wedding's association with family authority. The bride and groom greet each other with a mutual bow, a reciprocal bow of common greeting . . . , in contrast to the asymmetry of the bride's excessive prostrations in the [more traditional] Confucian rite" (66). As revealing as they are, the significance of changes such as these should not be overstated. As Kendall observes, processes of courtship, even when overseen or "jump started" by professional female matchmakers or female kin, make it crystal clear that women are chosen, that men do the choosing, and that these asymmetries suffuse bonds between husbands and wives and gender relations as a whole.

Processes involving the relative "dilution" and reworking through admixture of Korean Confucianism (as reflected in these passages) have thus been a mixed blessing for women. This is partly because these processes have been driven largely by economic and attendant forces such as urbanization and bureaucratization, which have simultaneously entailed the emergence of a new middle class, the development of widespread consumerism, rampant inflation, the commercialization and commodification of ritual, and burgeoning expectations that women should come to marriage with ever more lavish dowries. The burdensome dowry gifts (expensive wooden chests, "ritual silks," household goods, clothing, jewelry, and cash) that are now such a central feature of weddings, though rationalized as part of the Confucian past, are of relatively recent origin and were apparently never a defining feature of earlier forms of marriage. Perhaps even more oppressive is the fact that, while the most important criterion for matrimony for a man in present-day Korea is his earning capacity, for a woman it is her physical beauty and overall appearance, "a relentless standard of her worth and being" (Kendall 1996:94, 95)

The cultural emphasis on women's physical beauty has been a boon to cosmetic surgeons and the beauty and fashion industries in their entirety. I hasten to add that in their search for profits, new products, and ever expanding markets, these medical practitioners and industries have also been centrally involved in the creation and dissemination of cultural preoccupations with beauty in the first place, much like their counterparts in the West. In the late 1980s, 20 to 30 percent of unmarried Korean women in their early twenties had undergone plastic surgery to enhance the appearance of their eyes, noses, breasts, or other body parts (Kendall 1996:87 n. 2). This trend has since increased, driven partly by the proliferation in recent decades of new media products (e.g., fashion magazines for women), which are widely available at beauty parlors and in tea rooms and the homes and workplaces of friends and relatives. The magnitude of the increase may be gauged by a report released in 2004 by the Korean Ministry of Health and Welfare, which showed that 52.5 percent of the more than fifteen hundred female college students who were surveyed had undergone cosmetic surgery at least once (Keun-min 2005). Facts such as these are consistent with arguably more disturbing data indicating that four out of ten high school students in the capital city of Seoul express a desire for cosmetic surgery on purely aesthetic grounds (as distinct from medical necessity) (Duk-kun 2003).[9]

As in the West, the prevalence of cosmetic surgery is emblematic of the role of new technologies in the selection of women's body types and, indeed, in the care and management—including dispatching—of bodies in their entirety. So, too, is the widespread use of amniocentesis, ultrasound, sperm sorting, and other medical technologies to determine the sex of fetuses. The social and cultural dynamics conducive to favoring sons simultaneously involve discrimination against daughters, including daughters in utero. In many parts of Korea, the aborting of female fetuses (female-selective abortion) is quite common. Data bearing on the year 1993 "placed . . . Korea in the distinguished position of having the highest reported national sex ratio at birth in the world, at 115.6 boys per 100 girls" (Miller 2001:1084). Even when selective abortion of this nature does not occur, daughters have much less chance than sons of surviving infancy and the first few years of childhood. This is mainly because sons receive preferential treatment with respect to food, medicine, and care from their mothers and others involved in raising them, as has also been reported for China, Taiwan, and other parts of East Asia and for India, Bangladesh, and South Asia generally (Croll 2000: Miller 2001).

Sociohistorical trends of the sort outlined here are rarely uniform, unilinear, or monolithic. Thus, beginning in the 1980s many Koreans came to have negative views regarding recent developments in weddings and marriages. One objection centers around the idea that new-style weddings involve wasteful feasts and other frivolous expenditures. Others are more broadly construed, claiming that in their rush to "modernize" Koreans have taken on too many trappings of Western culture at the expense of valued traditions that are distinctively Korean and worthy of preservation on these grounds alone and a key source of social stability and moral guidance in a rapidly changing, unpredictable world. Because the observance and preservation of "tradition" in the domestic domain and beyond, especially in terms of clothing and sexual comportment, usually falls to women more than men, it should not be surprising to find that political and religious elites, advice columnists, and others tend to blame women for a broad range of Korea's social ills and the moral slide that is believed to have occasioned them. One series of critiques places the lion's share of the blame for the rampant materialism and individualism of the middle classes on "woman the consumer," as might be expected in light of the fact that women in Korea, as elsewhere, tend to be assigned tasks associated with maintaining, and ideally improving, the social standing of their families and households, "family status production work" in Hanna Papanek's (1979) terminology. "In the much transformed world of the new middle-class Korean family, housewives are intensely involved in family economic planning, dealings in real estate, and all manner of investment . . . , undertakings more likely to compromise the dignity of a middle-class Korean man" (Kendall 1996:218–19). These activities are usefully viewed in relation to women's predominance as matchmakers and shamans who "excel in domains of activity which demand an excruciating risk of face (*ch'emyon*) in the necessity of saying disagreeable things and ever having one's motives questioned". More generally, "Korean women make matches, make marriages, make money, make rituals for the spirits; and all these activities fall under the shadow of disapprobation." Why? Because "money lending and real estate dealings are sordid and avaricious, religious activities are superstitious and sometimes disreputable, celebrations and ceremonious exchanges have the potential to become an unwholesome extravagance, a source of intrafamilial strife, and a target of reformist campaigns" (218–19).

In the past few decades, increasing numbers of Koreans have come to feel that myriad aspects of their culture are destined for the trash bins of history unless active steps are taken to "stem the tide." These sentiments led to the creation in 1974 of the Institute of Decorum and Wisdom (known as Yejiwon), a "finishing school" established to train the daughters of elites in the proper ways of "being Korean." Since elite families were stewards of the cultural traditions of earlier generations of nobility that had come to signify "Koreanness," in 1983 the institute added a bridal course to its curriculum. This course presently involves three meetings a week for a period of three months, during which time young women "learn how to arrange flowers, how to make tea, how to wear traditional Korean dress and how to behave at funerals. Some lessons focus on relations with mothers-in-law, couples psychology, childbirth and cooking. Etiquette experts point out how to maintain decorum, how to walk and bow, and how to adopt appropriate facial expressions" (Onishi 2004). The institute's founder and director, Kang Yong Sook, explained that other topics of instruction involve "Western and Chinese cooking, and Western manners as well, to align with the globalized society we live in" (ibid).

What the founder and director of the Institute of Decorum and Wisdom did not say is that the poorest segments of Korean society are much less likely to be able to afford marriage and legitimate biological and social reproduction. These differentials exemplify dynamics of "stratified reproduction." This term was developed by Shellee Cohen (1995) in the context of the contemporary United States to refer to the encompassing systems of power relations that facilitate certain groups' nurturance and reproduction while discouraging or precluding those of others. Such systems of stratified reproduction are widespread both in Asia and in other parts of the world.

Romance as a National Security Issue (Singapore)

Koreans are by no means alone in feeling that the dynamics of courtship, romance, and all that might follow are too important to be left to inexperienced and untutored youth. In early 2003, government officials in the Southeast Asian (but predominantly Chinese) nation of Singapore, increasingly alarmed about the long-term implications of the country's low birthrate, launched a nationwide campaign "to encourage people to fall in love, marry and start families."[10] Aided by private businesses and "timed to coincide with Valentine's Day," which is observed by many youth in the cosmopolitan city-state (and in Japan and other parts of Asia),[11] this initiative involved state-sponsored "dances, concerts, drive-in movies and other activities aimed at putting people 'in the right mood for love.'" As with similar moves in previous decades (Heng and Devan 1995), the action was prompted by the release of figures indicating a plummeting birthrate, specifically that the year 2002 saw only 40,800 births in a country whose overall population at the time was about 4.4 million. This was both a fourteen-year low and well below "the rate needed for the natural replacement of the population, making Singapore increasingly dependent on foreign labor and raising the specter of an aging population and higher social welfare costs." It is difficult to know if the low birth rate reflects "a prolonged economic slump in the city-state, including a severe economic recession in 2001" or other variables. But some Singaporeans feel that cultural factors are at least partly responsible.

To provide some background, in the early years following the attainment of independence in 1965, Singapore's ruling party, the People's Action Party (PAP) realized that it needed to devise strategies to accommodate and manage the exceedingly high population densities that would likely be a permanent feature of the future. (The 2005 population density was approximately 6,667 persons per square kilometer, comparable to that of San Francisco and about two-thirds that of New York City.) It settled on the idea of constructing blocks of "public" high-rise apartment buildings that would be owned and managed by the state. This would serve the dual purpose of housing citizen-subjects and helping to guarantee their loyalty to state policies and their employers alike. Since the state effectively monopolizes the entire housing market (roughly 86 percent of the resident population lives in state housing [PuruShotam 1998:138]), opposition to state policies can bring eviction and an inability to obtain housing in the future. In turn, disloyalty to one's employer or uneven job performance can result in loss of the job necessary to make housing payments. There is an additional downside to these arrangements from the point of view of young people, one that occurs in one form or another in many other areas of the world: young adults of working age cannot afford to "strike out on their own" and must continue to live with their parents, unmarried siblings, and in some cases grandparents until they marry. Some observers might see in these living arrangements evidence of "strong family ties'" or "Asian values," but a realistic complaint relayed by one Singaporean, Dr. Wei Siang Yu, is that if we "move out only when . . . [we] get married, . . . "how am I going to have sex? How am I going to bring a girl [or boy] home?"

Another factor that some Singaporeans see as relevant to the worrisome decline in birthrates (especially among the city's Chinese) has to do with the highly competitive ethos and attendant "feeling-tones" that are simultaneously demanded and rewarded in the workplace and society at large. These cultural orientations discourage the display of feelings and any evidence of "softness," which is gendered and "racialized" and thus avoided for a variety of reasons. Malays and Indians, who are defined in Singapore as separate "races," make up roughly 22 percent of Singapore's multiethnic population, occupy the lowest rungs of the socioeconomic ladder, and are commonly depicted in nationalist discourses as soft, feminine, and threatening to the predominantly Chinese/ Confucian "national fiber." Hence, under one or another guise, state policies seek to promote "Chineseness" and to distance Chinese and non-Chinese alike from the cultural orientations of the soft races, which threaten continued prosperity and progress—another form of stratified reproduction.

Since 1984, the government has been involved in the business of matchmaking, prompted by declines in family size and concerns over the ever increasing numbers of single professionals who are postponing marriage and perhaps (to the alarmists) forgoing it altogether. One initiative involved the creation of the Social Development Unit, a dating agency for those with university degrees, which "matches Singaporeans with university degrees who have little time—or aptitude—for finding romantic partners." Additionally, in 2001, "the government started a program to encourage couples to have two or more children by offering a 'baby bonus' package of financial and educational incentives. Singles who prefer conventional face-to-face dates can turn to an eight-page dating manual, 'When Boy Meets Girl! The Chemistry Guide,' produced by the government" in 2002. Other advice included useful tips such as: "A date is very similar to a job interview. You have to sell yourself. People are drawn to good listeners. But don't just sit there passively; engage whomever you are with." Reports describing these activities in 2003 noted that in order

> to put these guidelines into practice, singles attend activities planned by the Premier Club, which has been organizing dining, traveling and exercise sessions for the Social Development Unit's 20,000 members since April 2001. The club has also put together events like "Speed Dating" and "Blind Dates." In speed dating,

couples have seven minutes to get to know one another before they move on to the next person. So far Premier has held 130 sessions, and about three out of four singles leave with at least one match.

Such national campaigns might seem relatively positive or benign. But they have a dark side: political elites and those in the state-controlled media and elsewhere who do their bidding for them have mobilized formal and informal sanctions to ostracize and stigmatize those who fail to take the bait or are disqualified on one or more grounds from enjoying the fruits of the campaigns. These sanctions include de facto financial penalties for those who fail to qualify for the incentives, discrimination, and discipline and surveillance of various kinds, as well as mass-mediated ostracism. Most directly targeted for stigmatization and discrimination are university-educated, middle-class, and professional Chinese women who postpone or rule out "serious" dating and courtship that might lead to marriage, conception, pregnancy, and child-rearing, and those who marry but choose not to have children right away, or at all, or have them in "insufficient" numbers. Also targeted are women, and to a lesser extent men, who act on or harbor (but for fear of reprisals do not actually go public with) desires to be in relationships with others of the same sex. In Singapore, as in Taiwan and elsewhere, these campaigns and the discourses giving rise to them "work against women's [and men's] same-sex desire, not only by denouncing and prohibiting it, but also by silencing it, erasing it, rendering it unthinkable, invisible, and insignificant" (Sang 2003:232). More generally, Singapore's battle for the hearts and minds of the new middle classes is predicated on a system of stratified reproduction similar to what we saw in Korea. There are significant contrasts, however, because ethnic and class differences in Singapore are mapped onto one another in ways that do not occur, or are far less pronounced, in the more ethnically homogeneous Korea.

Of key relevance in the Singaporean context is a trio of explicitly articulated presumptions that has been elevated to the status of a national credo and has been more or less sanctified along the way. The first of these presumptions entails the now "commonsense" view that it is necessary and desirable to keep the city-state from sliding back toward its unsavory colonial era past, which was characterized by crushing poverty, widespread disease, malnutrition, hunger, arranged marriages, polygynous unions, concubinage, large households, and degrading female servitude. The second presumption has to do with the need to ensure Singapore's continued development and march toward progress—"a better tomorrow," which requires that everyone take their place in a "normal family" consisting of husband, wife, and children. The third is that each of these natural units is and must be ruled by a patriarch in accordance with "ancient Chinese (Confucian) custom" (PuruShotam 1998).

No matter that "[s]ome of the . . . 'families'" living in Singapore prior to the 1960s clearly "contradicted the norms of heterosexuality and patriarchy" inasmuch as they involved either "Fukien-derived practice[s] of male homosexuality and male-male marriages" or "Canton-derived associations of women entering into lesbian marriages" (PuruShotam 1998:135, Topley 1959) or that same-sex relations in imperial China were not universally stigmatized and in some contexts were viewed in positive terms (Sang 2003:55–56 passim; Greenberg 1988:161, 440). Archival and other material relevant to Singapore's past reveals a panoply of housing and domestic arrangements and many different forms of sociality and intimacy (Warren [1986] 2003, 1993), a wide variety of which exist at present, in some cases as "open secrets," in other instances largely underground. Writing about Chinese in another diasporic context, San Francisco in the late nineteenth and early twentieth centuries, Nayan Shah (2001) subsumes all such social arrangements and relations of intimacy under the rubric of "queer domesticity." He does so partly to highlight their departures from contemporary norms and partly to reclaim their validity and legitimacy, much as some gay and lesbian activists have done with the term "queer."

The overdetermined emphasis in present-day Singapore on "the normal," on what Michel Foucault ([1984] 1997; cf. 1977, 1978) refers to as "normativity," highlights some of the slippage, ambiguity, and euphemized violence entailed in the merging and elision of two very different meanings of the concept of "normal" (and "norm"). On the one hand, the term "normal" designates what is statistically normal or common, or routinely present, in a quantifiable sense. On the other hand, it refers to what is morally acceptable as when the root "norm" is preceded by the term "moral" to produce "moral norm(s)." A recurrent theme in Foucault's influential scholarship concerns the emergence in the West, beginning in the eighteenth and nineteenth centuries, of "routine" scientific examinations in schools, hospitals, clinics, asylums, army barracks, prisons, and other institutional settings so as to establish statistical commonalities (means, medians, norms, and averages) and departures from them. This development went hand in hand with the rise in sophisticated technologies and regimes of discipline, surveillance, and control that political and religious elites drew upon to discern and/or create statistical norms that resonated with their views as to what is morally normal and enjoined, and vice versa. All else was decreed to be beyond the pale and was dealt with accordingly by the production of societal discourses and the attendant marshaling of sanctions of the sort for which Singapore is justly notorious.

The Singaporean ideology of the "normal family," seen by ruling elites since the 1980s as necessary to help launch and sustain the new Asian capitalisms, is grounded in racialist discourses of "ancient Chineseness," unilineal notions of "development" as "progress," and narratives of gender and the life course that focus on the "natural," normal unfolding of lives in the context of a strictly disciplined domesticity: "Girls will become young women who will marry, produce children and raise them. These are their central tasks," which revolve around their role "as mothers, the creators and protectors of the next generation", to quote from one of then Prime Minister Lee Kuan Yew's (in)famous 1983 speeches on the subject (PuruShotam 1998:142). "Boys will grow up and marry too, but their familial responsibility is as breadwinners . . . [T]heir major concern is to engage in the public world . . . [and] they are . . . the natural heads of their families" (135).

Women are clearly subordinated by the terms of patriarchy. According to Lee's successor, Goh Chok Tong, their access to various "rights, benefits and privileges" should only come "through the head of the family, so that he can enforce the obligations and responsibilities of family members'" (PuruShotam 1998:143). But, as is repeatedly emphasized by political elites and the state-controlled media, women have it much better than before. This is due to the policies of the state, which is cast as a strict but caring and omniscient father figure that helped democratize kinship and marriage relations and allowed the majority of Singaporeans to attain middle-class standing. The fruits of such policies are constructed as gifts to the citizenry ("the children") who are expected to reciprocate with unwavering loyalty and obedience. The state's "gifts" to its daughters thus necessitate their continued obedience to the state and its proxies, and those designated as their guardians and protectors, along with their acceptance of certain basic "facts." As Goh has insisted, "women must accept that they live in a patriarchal society and should realize that it is 'not possible nor is it wise to have total sex equality in all areas'" (143).

Women's demands for equality are commonly trivialized by opponents of women's rights. Alternatively, they are written off as either "opposition for the sake of opposition" or indulgence stemming from uncritical acceptance of Western-style political agendas that are ill-suited to the cultural-historical and geopolitical environment of Singapore, a prosperous but geographically tiny island that will forever be subject to threats and destabilizing influences of external origin beyond its control. The siege mentality fostered by the government promotes a climate in which "wrong choices," especially choices made by middle-class and professional Chinese women to postpone or forgo marriage or child rearing, could "destroy all that has been gained thus far . . . and inhibit forward momentum" (PuruShotam 1998:132–33). "If women do not do the right thing as women, then our economy will falter, the administration will suffer, and the society will decline" (Lee Kuan Yew 1983, cited in PuruShotam 1998:164). The "fear of falling" thus instilled in the populace targets women, scapegoating—and defining as un-Asian—those who fail to toe the line in terms of heterosexual marriage and childbearing, since "to reject the ['normal'] Asian family is . . . to reject Asian culture" (151–52).

Nirmala PuruShotam (1998:160), an expert on Singapore, notes: "It is no coincidence that the elite's concerns about the continuation of the middle-class way of life, as it has been reproduced thus far, takes women as its main subjects and objects of social control." For women "bring with them the spectre of individual choice, individual rights, individualism *per se*, in a political context that not only openly dismisses the individualist conceptualization of people as irrelevant, even dangerous, but which also embraces a highly particularised notion of communitarian democracy." The more general pattern we see in Singapore and most other parts of the world is that those holding positions of power and prestige typically blame women for the real and imagined problems associated with social change. This is but one of many forms of discrimination that women encounter.

Favoring Sons, Discriminating against Daughters (South Asia and East Asia)

In order to understand Asian patterns of discrimination against women, we need to bear in mind that most, if not all, Asian societies define adulthood in social rather than physiological terms. To be considered an adult, it is usually necessary to be (or to have once been) married and to have given birth to, fathered, or adopted one or more children.[12] The strong expectation that virtually everyone will marry and have children reflects a number of values and interests, including the hope that children will take care of their parents during old age and continue the household and ancestral line. The relative prevalence throughout Asia of systems of patrilineal descent and inheritance is coupled with patrilocal postmarital residence, which means that once they are married sons tend to reside in or near their parents' residential compounds and villages. The earning potential of sons usually exceeds that of daughters because of inequitable gendered divisions of labor in the household and discrimination against women in the paid labor force. Thus, sons are more likely to be in a position to help take care of their parents when the parents are old and infirm and to have the resources necessary to sponsor rituals geared toward honoring the ancestors and spirits linked to the household and the kin group(s) associated with it.

In these settings, which are common throughout China, Taiwan, Japan, Korea, Vietnam, India, Pakistan, and Bangladesh, daughters, unlike sons, move away upon marriage and are otherwise seen as representing a net economic loss to their natal households as well as the families and larger kin groups into which they were born. "Metaphorically, they . . . [are] little birds destined to fly away—as one poignant [Rajasthani] wedding song puts it" (Raheja and Gold 1994:xxxii). The costs to parents of marrying off daughters also greatly exceed the expenses involved in arranging and celebrating sons' marriages. This is partly because both customary and modern-day marriage payments from the parents and other kin of the bride to the bridal couple (dowry) and/or the groom's family (groomwealth) greatly exceed those that flow in the opposite direction (from the parents and other kin of the groom to the bridal couple and/or the bride's kin, e.g., bridewealth). Due to the fact that marriage payments index shifting prestige hierarchies and a wide variety of status considerations, including concerns with moving up in status hierarchies and anxieties about sliding down, they are subject to notoriously inflationary spirals. Parents and other family members bear the material and psychological burdens of these spirals, which can be enormous.

Circumstances such as these, which are reinforced by religious ideologies that accord males more prestige than females, help explain why in many Asian societies sons are strongly favored over daughters. The favoring of sons typically involves one or more forms of active or passive discrimination against daughters, the most common being (1) the aborting of female fetuses (also known as female-selective abortion); (2) female infanticide (also known as female-selective infanticide); and (3) the intentional, as well as more or less unconscious, diverting of resources—food, medicine, and the care and supervision provided by parents, elder siblings, and others—from daughters to sons. In certain parts of Asia, particularly Korea, China, Taiwan, Vietnam, India, Pakistan, and Bangladesh, these forms of discrimination have resulted in sex ratios that are extremely unbalanced—so much so that the Indian economist Amartya Sen and various other scholars, when speaking of women and girls in Asia, have referred to the "missing millions" (Miller 2001:1090). Owing to the increasingly widespread availability of medical technology that can easily and inexpensively determine the sex of a fetus (through amniocentesis, ultrasound, sperm sorting, and the like), estimates published in early 2006 indicate that some ten million female fetuses were aborted in India alone over the past two decades (Jha et al. 2006).

In terms of national averages, Korea, as noted earlier, enjoys the dubious distinction of having the most skewed sex ratios at birth, with 115.6 boys per 100 girls (according to 1993 data). China weighed in at 114 boys per 100 girls in 1989, though, as elsewhere, this overall figure obscures the prevalence of female-selective abortion in the case of second, third, and fourth births: "121 for second-order births, 124 for third-order births, and 132 for fourth-order births" (Miller 2001:1084). Data from

India indicated 112 boys per 100 girls in the early 1990s, though here, too, regional variations are quite pronounced, with some parts of India reporting considerably higher skewing, much like Pakistan, the national figures for which indicate "very high sex ratios for first births: 137 in 1986, 116 in 1987, 133 in 1988, 124 in 1989, and 117 in 1990" (1086). To convey a sense of what these figures mean, the anthropologist and demographer Barbara Miller explains that a sex ratio at birth "of 117–120 boys per 100 girls, for example, means that . . . one of every seven-to-ten female fetuses has been selectively aborted" (1084).

The favoring of sons via female-selective abortion in South Asian settings such as India, Pakistan, and Bangladesh tends to be less pronounced among Muslims than Hindus. According to Miller, the main reason for this is rather straightforward: Muslims are more likely than Hindus to view all forms of abortion as proscribed by religion. Worthy of mention as well is that female-selective abortion tends to be largely absent in Southeast Asia, with the notable exception of Vietnam, whose rates of abortion may exceed those of any other country in Asia.[13] This pattern probably reflects a greater degree of egalitarianism in gender relations -- along with the relatively rarity of patriliny (except, again, in Vietnam) compared with world areas such as South Asia and East Asia. In some regions of Muslim Southeast Asia, such as the state of Negeri Sembilan, Malaysia, parents commonly express a preference for daughters over sons (Peletz 1996:220–21). This preference, however, does not entail male-selective abortion or the severe resource diversion toward favored children that one sees in Korea, China, India, Pakistan, and so on. Preferences such as these tend to be articulated by villagers (women and men alike) living in rural communities in which matriliny and matrilocality have long been prevalent. In these settings, recall, descent is traced through women and upon marriage men move from their natal compounds and villages and join their wives. Here daughters are accorded key features of the caretaking and provisioning roles assigned to sons elsewhere (e.g., in patrilineal, patrilocal settings). In these societies, daughters and women generally are not accorded more prestige than sons or men as a whole, but there is more equality than in their South and East Asian counterparts.

Observers have long assumed that female-selective abortion and other forms of discrimination against daughters would fade with modernization, but this has proven not to be the case. Indeed, there is evidence of a rise in female-selective abortion in numerous parts of South and East Asia due largely to increases in the cost of children's marriages, especially the marriages of daughters, coupled with the availability of new technology (Miller 2001). Perhaps even more surprising is the fact that in some regions the parents who are most likely to resort to female-selective abortion belong to the relatively well-off and educated classes. These are the parents who face the largest and most inflation-prone expenses in marrying off their daughters. One way in which parents endeavor to cope with the expenditures and inflationary spirals at issue here is to abort female fetuses.

3

Bodies, Pleasures, and Desires: Transgender Practices, Same-Sex Relations, and Heteronormative Sexualities

Much of the discussion thus far has focused on kinship, marriage, household organization, and the hegemonic forms of gender and sexuality that prevail in modern Asian societies. The hegemonic expressions of gender and sexuality we have examined are sometimes referred to as "heteronormative." This term emphasizes the heterosexual relations and desires that are normative for the majority of the population in the sense that they are (1) enjoined upon them by means of institutionalized moral expectations that are internalized, more often than not unconsciously, as sentiments, dispositions, and embodied practices through the socialization process and the structures and lived experiences of everyday life; and (2) statistically prevalent throughout society.

Gender and sexual diversity also exists within—and not merely across —specific societies, including societies informed by one or another type of heteronormativity. This section engages that diversity, focusing mainly on same-sex relations and transgender practices and identities. We shall see that there is considerable variation in Asian societies with respect to the ways in which non-normative expressions of gender and sexuality are conceptualized by society, and that the status accorded individuals involved in same-sex relations and transgender practices varies a great deal from one society to the next. In certain cases, such individuals are revered, even held to be sacred. In others, they are both stigmatized and criminalized. The larger point is that in some societies sentiments and dispositions bearing on gender and sexuality are characterized by a fair degree of pluralism, whereas in other societies pluralism is highly attenuated at best.

Especially in recent years, scholars have spilled much ink on the pros and cons of the different terminological conventions that might be used to refer to institutionalized roles and identities that involve one or another type of departure or deviation from gender normativity. Along with other scholars, I use the umbrella term "transgender" for this purpose, even though it is employed by different scholars in different ways.[1] I take my reading of the prefix "trans" from Aihwa Ong (1999:4), who has written, "*Trans* denotes both moving through space or across lines, as well as changing the nature of something"—as in transformation or transfiguration or, going beyond this, transcend—be it a bounded entity or process or a relationship between two or more phenomena. Concerning transgender, Riki Wilchins (1997:15-16) has observed that "Transgender began its life as a name for those folks who identified neither as crossdressers nor as transsexuals—primarily people who changed their gender but not their genitals . . . The term gradually mutated to include any genderqueers who didn't actually change their genitals: [such as] crossdressers, . . . stone butches, and hermaphrodites; . . . [and] people began using it to refer to transsexuals [some of whom do change their genitals] as well." Evelyn Blackwood's (1999, 2005) conceptualization of transgender builds on Wilchins' definition, though she also employs the term transgendered in its broadest sense to refer to anyone who is "transgressively gendered," to borrow Kate Bornstein's (1995:134–35) phrase.

Many scholars underscore that in some Western contexts these umbrella terms have certain meanings and connotations that are of questionable relevance elsewhere. Such meanings and connotations include the empirically erroneous idea that all variants of transgendering necessarily entail same-sex relations (and vice versa). They also include the equally problematic notion that behavioral transgressions, even or especially in the straightforward definitional sense of practices that transcend or cross boundaries (bearing on gender or anything else), are typically stigmatized. So we must utilize the terms with caution when we are labeling, grouping, and interpreting practices and identities in Asian settings.

A final remark has to do with the term "pluralism". I use this term to refer to social fields, cultural domains, and more encompassing systems in which two or more principles, categories, groups, sources of authority, or ways of being in the world are not only present, tolerated, and accommodated but also *accorded legitimacy* in a basic Weberian sense (Deveaux 2000; Jost and Major 2001). Legitimacy is thus a sine qua non for pluralism, which means by definition that pluralism is a feature of fields, domains, and systems in which diversity is ascribed legitimacy, and, conversely, that diversity without legitimacy is not pluralism.

Pluralism in gendered fields or domains, here abbreviated as "gender pluralism," includes pluralistic sensibilities and dispositions regarding bodily practices (adornment, dress, mannerisms) and embodied desires, as well as social roles, sexual relationships, and overall ways of being that bear on or are otherwise linked with local conceptions of femininity, masculinity, androgyny, and so on. Particularly in gendered fields and domains, pluralism transcends and must be distinguished from dualism inasmuch as more than two principles, categories and groups are usually at sake and accorded legitimacy (e.g., not simply principles constituting categories of heteronormative female-bodied individuals and their male-bodied counterparts). Under this definition, sexual pluralism, premised minimally on a concept of relatively "benign sexual variation" (Rubin 1984:283), is included under the more encompassing rubric of gender pluralism.

"Neither Man Nor Woman" (India in Comparative Perspective)

South Asia, like Southeast Asia and Native North America, is one of many world areas with long-established traditions of ritual specialists who engage in transgender practices. These individuals either assume the attire, occupations, demeanor, and (sometimes) erotic orientations of members of the "opposite" sex or engage in one or another set of practices that result in their being considered by others in the society as a "third sex" or "third gender" (and sometimes, as in the case of female-bodied transgenderists in certain Native American societies, a fourth gender). In precontact Native North America, for example, there appear to have been more than 155 distinct societies with these traditions (Roscoe 1998:7). In most of those societies, the "two-spirit people," or *berdache*, as they are sometimes called, were male-bodied individuals—although in "about a third of these groups" two-spirit roles existed for phenotypic females as well (7)—who were held to have unique spiritual powers, sometimes revealed to them in dreams, which provided them with an important source of prestige in their communities. As for their domestic arrangements and erotic orientations, a two-spirit person typically engaged in sexual relations and marriage perhaps best summarized as both homosexual and heterogender: a male-bodied two spirit, for example, typically married and had sexual relations with another person having male genitals who was gendered male, unlike the two spirit, who was regarded not as a male (despite having male genitals) but as a "woman-man" or "man-woman" and hence a third gender. These relations were thus homosexual from the (culturally muted) anatomical point of view but heterogender in terms of the way the individuals involved were gendered.

Broadly similar ritual roles keyed to homosexual/heterogender matrices have existed in Southeast Asia for many centuries (e.g., among Bugis, Iban, Ngaju Dayak, Javanese, Filipinos, Burmese, and many others [Peletz 2006, forthcoming]), though to my knowledge no one has enumerated precisely how many there were. In these Southeast Asian cases, the ritual specialists in question combined elements from and simultaneously transcended the male-female duality that helped structure and animate the universe in its entirety and simultaneously symbolized wholeness, purity, and gender totality and thus the unfractured universe posited to exist before the advent of humanity and difference (Errington 1989; L. Andaya 2000). In many of the cosmologies of the region, important spirits and deities were depicted as exhibiting various degrees of androgyny or as existing in male-female pairs (grandfather and grandmother, husband and wife, or brother and sister). Ritual specialists exhibiting androgyny were ideally situated to both communicate and successfully negotiate with these spirits and deities and to personify them.

In South Asia, the best-documented examples of what many scholars and local populations alike consider a "third sex" are known as *hijra*s (see, e.g., Nanda 1990, 1993; L. Cohen 1995; Agrawal 1997; and Reddy 2005). This term refers to castelike groups of ritual specialists composed of hermaphrodites as well as males who have had their penis and testes sacrificially excised and have thus become eunuchs, the latter making up the *hijra* majority. *Hijra*s dress and adorn themselves as women; adopt stereotypically (often exaggerated) female hand gestures, gait, and overall demeanor; engage in female domestic activities such as cooking, sewing, sweeping, and cleaning; and behave like women in various other ways, though they also have a reputation for being louder and more verbally aggressive than ordinary women. For at least a thousand years, *hijra*s have existed in Hindu communities in India and since the sixteenth century, if not earlier, among Muslims as well, performing sacred roles that have included maintaining temples devoted to deities associated with the Mother Goddess as well as dancing, playing music, and conducting various ritual services at weddings and the births of male children, events that are among the most joyous and significant ceremonial occasions for Hindus and Muslims throughout India and South Asia as a whole.

The role and social standing of *hijra*s in contemporary India is complex and fraught, as are the quotidian negotiations of *hijra* identity both within their own communities and in relation to the larger society. British colonial policies bear some responsibility for this situation in that they criminalized castration, defined all eunuchs as dangerous outlaws, and otherwise denigrated the role. So, too, does the fact that many *hijra*s no longer maintain the celibacy and asceticism that were long seen as defining features of their identities (Reddy 2005:26–28 passim). In many cases, moreover, impoverished *hijra*s have turned to prostitution with non-*hijra*, sometimes heterosexually identified, married males to support themselves, contributing to dissension and strife among *hijra*s as to the proper way to comport oneself and enhance, or at least maintain, one's honor or respect (*izzat*) and adding to the ambivalence with which they are viewed by the general public. *Hijra*s are nonetheless accorded an important degree of legitimacy and sanctity by society at large. This is largely because of the valuable rituals they perform, as well as their identification in India's public culture both with "Bahuchara Mata, one of the many versions of the Mother Goddess worshipped throughout India," and with a strongly androgynous, if not bisexual, form of "the sexually ambivalent Siva" (Nanda 1993:373, 375).

To understand how the Hindu majority conceptualizes *hijra*s and their spiritual powers, we need to bear in mind four sets of issues. First, in Hinduism "'male' and 'female' are seen as natural categories in complementary opposition," each of which is "naturally" associated with "different sexual characteristics and reproductive organs, . . . different sexual natures . . . and . . . different, and complementary, roles in marriage, sexual relations and reproduction" (Nanda 1993:374). Second, the female principle, which is "more immanent and active" than the male principle, "has a positive, creative, life-giving aspect and a destructive life-destroying aspect." In numerous contexts, "the erotic aspect of female power is dangerous unless it is controlled by the male principle," which is why many (but not all) Hindus and scholars of Hinduism believe that "powerful women, whether deities or humans, must be restrained by male authority. Thus the Hindu goddess subordinated to her male consort is beneficent, but when dominant the goddess" may be "aggressive, devouring and destructive" (374), at least with respect to demonic enemies, in which case she may still be a savior of humans and male deities.[2] Third, just as many Hindu deities are "sexually ambiguous," often being depicted in myth, ritual, and iconography in androgynous or dual-gendered forms, so, too, do many of them change over time, from largely male to predominantly female and vice versa, for instance, and/or from one to many and back again. The fourth point (which follows partly from the others) is that spiritual salvation presupposes transcendence and change, and, more generally, that Hinduism's doctrinal emphasis on rebirth, variability, and multiplicity serves both to valorize mutability and transformation and to underscore their intrinsic connections with spiritual potency.

As for issues of identity and subjectivity, most individuals who become *hijra*s do so through surgical removal of the penis and testes—which, in the case of effeminate boys encouraged by their parents to join the ranks of *hijra*s around the time of puberty, may occur while they are in their early teens—not because they were born intersexed (hermaphroditic). It is partly for this reason that, even when they view themselves as "neither man nor woman" or "man plus woman," *hijra*s sometimes consider themselves more male than female. Because *hijra*s lack male genitalia, as well as sexual desire for women, in some contexts they think of themselves as "not male," "less than male," or as "incomplete males." Because they are not endowed with female sexual organs or the capacity to bear children but dress and adorn themselves like women and perform various female tasks, in other contexts they regard themselves as "incomplete women" rather than in terms of one or another category defined in relation to masculinity or its lack (not male, less than male, etc.). It is important to underscore that these identities, all of which bear on ostensibly bedrock "sexual(ized) difference," are not the only, or necessarily the most personally or culturally salient, identities negotiated by *hijra*s. As with those of other Hindus and Muslims in modern India, *hijra*s' subjectivities and senses of self are informed in complex, sometimes contradictory ways by a panoply of factors. These include their religious affiliations, relative piety, and place of birth; the linguistic communities to which they belong; their past and present involvement in networks of kinship, romance, and desire; the extent to which they honor one or another vow of asceticism or world renunciation (or have done so in the past); their ritual and artistic specializations, educational attainment, occupational activities, employment status, and overall socioeconomic standing; and, last but not least, their familiarity with and, where relevant, their self-positioning in relation to Indian-inflected global discourses bearing on the meaning of terms such as "homosex" and "gay" (Reddy 2005:74–76 passim).

Conceptualizations of *hijra*s along with the construction and entailments of the *hijra* role make it clear that some Asian societies regard sexuality and gender as fluid, permeable, even hybrid categories that are contextually specific and subject to combination, flux, and change. The *hijra* example also illustrates that some Asian societies do not insist that at birth every individual be assigned a lifelong sexual designation or gender role derived from a system composed of two rigidly defined sex/gender categories and, more generally, that not all societies operate with a binary system based on two sexes or genders. It merits note, finally, that, while modern-day *hijra*s tend to be viewed by normative Hindus and Muslims with ambivalence and are in some instances apparently less revered than stigmatized and feared (owing to their spiritual potency and tendencies to threaten with misfortune those who cross them), they differ from their gender-transgressive counterparts in the West in that they are accorded a meaningful and seemingly fulfilling role that is both legitimate and in some ways sanctified.

Transgender practices involving female-bodied individuals exist in India as well, but they are not "as widespread, visible, or prominent as the *hijra*s" (Nanda 2000:40). One type of female-bodied transgenderism involves female ascetics known as *sadhin*s (a feminine form of the Hindi term for holy man, *sadhu*), who take vows of lifelong celibacy around or ideally before the onset of puberty and thus renounce all forms of sexuality as well as marriage (since marriage typically involves sexuality). This variant of transgenderism is far more limited in both its distribution and its antiquity than transgenderism of the *hijra* variety, just as female renunciation is relatively rare in India compared to male renunciation, though each occurs in many forms (Denton 2004; Khandelwal 2004; Khandelwal et al. 2006). The *sadhin* role probably originated in the final decades of the nineteenth century and is largely confined to a small ethnic group known as Gaddis whose members live in the foothills of the Himalayas in Northwest India (Phillimore 1991). They are primarily pastoralists, but their economy is a mixture of animal herding and agriculture.

In accordance with their renunciation of normative female sexuality and many other defining features of conventional femininity, *sadhin*s don the clothing and adopt the hairstyles of men. They may participate in occupational activities normally reserved for men (herding sheep, processing wool, and plowing), though they also perform women's work. "On gender-segregated ceremonial occasions, adult *sadhin*s may sit with the men as well as smoke the water pipe and cigarettes, definitely masculine behaviors. Yet [a] *sadhin* do[es] not generally attend funerals, a specifically male prerogative" (Nanda 2000:40–41), retains her original female name, is referred to and addressed with female kin terms, and is "never classified socially as a male," being considered instead an "as if" or "virtual" male as well as an as if or virtual ascetic (Phillimore 1991:337, 341).

Serena Nanda (2000:41), one of the foremost experts on gender diversity in India, emphasizes that "unlike *hijra*s, . . . *sadhin*s have no special ritual or performance roles in society, nor are they considered to have any special sacred powers" other than those associated with their asceticism. That said, their asceticism is more partial than that of *hijra*s and male ascetics who, unlike *sadhin*s, "transcend sex/gender classification and can renounce the world at any age or stage of life." Because a female-bodied individual who seeks to be an ascetic is generally expected to renounce sexuality and marriage before puberty in order to be accepted by society as a *sadhin*, Nanda has suggested that "within orthodox Hinduism, the *sadhin* role is a way of controlling female sexuality and providing a social niche for the woman who rejects the only legitimate female roles in traditional Hindu India, those of wife and mother." More broadly, "because a woman's decision to reject marriage is an unacceptable challenge . . . among orthodox Hindus, the *sadhin* role, defined as an asexual female gender variant, acts as a constraint on the potential, unacceptable sexuality of unmarried women" (41). In the words of the anthropologist Peter Phillimore (1991:347), who has conducted extensive fieldwork among the Gaddis, their "cultural creativity . . . [in] convert[ing] the negative associations of spinsterhood into the positive associations of *sadhin*-hood . . . entails nothing less than the denial of sexuality to these individuals, by classing them as asexual. Such is the price paid for social legitimacy and relative day-to-day autonomy."

Summarizing the most general lessons one might draw from these two Indian cases, we might say, following Nanda, that "The *sadhin* role provides one kind of response to the cultural challenge of adult female virginity in a society where marriage and motherhood are the dominant feminine ideals." The *hijra* role, on the other hand, "despite its many contradictions, gives meaning and even power to male sex/gender ambiguity in a highly patriarchal culture. While all cultures must deal with those whose anatomy or behavior leaves them outside the classification of male and female, man and woman, it is the genius of Hinduism [and Indian Islam] that allows for so many different ways of being human" (2000:41).

Toms, Dees, and Gender-Transgressive Males (Thailand, Indonesia, and the Philippines)

Transgender practices and same-sex relations in Thailand, Indonesia, the Philippines, and other regions of Southeast Asia tend to be accorded a greater degree of legitimacy and are in other respects different from their counterparts in South Asian as well as East Asian settings. The greater degree of legitimacy they enjoy is in keeping with the fact that, broadly speaking, Southeast Asian societies have long evinced less patriarchy and a greater degree of pluralism with respect to gender and sexuality than have neighboring world areas. It is beyond the scope of this discussion to explain why this is so, but relevant factors include the bilateral systems of descent and inheritance coupled with matrifocal (mother-centered) emphases and matrilocal/neolocal postmarital residence patterns characteristic of Southeast Asia, as distinct from the patrilineal/patrifocal/patrilocal traditions prevalent in South Asia and East Asia; the relatively low population densities and more favorable distributions of resources long typical of Southeast Asia; the relatively weak state structures characteristic of Southeast Asia during the early modern period (and before); differences in systems of production, exchange, and personhood; and last, but not least, the salience of Indicized but uniquely Southeast Asian mythologies and cosmologies in providing templates for gender and sexuality throughout the region. Many Southeast Asian systems of myth, ritual, and cosmology encourage imaginative play conducive to the creation of implicit cultural models valorizing relativism, pluralism, and different ways of being in the world that allow for a variety of "potentially erotic enterprises" (Butler 1993:110).

Some argue that what sets Southeast Asia apart from South and East Asia and many other places, and simultaneously renders it broadly analogous to certain regions of Native North America in former times, is not that gender-transgressive practices were construed as legitimate in particular contexts, for such phenomena have long been evident in many world areas and they continue to exist in the contemporary United States (e.g., in Ivy League clubs and northern California's infamous Bohemian Grove).³ Rather, what is distinctive about Southeast Asia is that compared to other world areas the pluralism-friendly dynamics in question were *not* bracketed exceptions to the prevailing hegemonies, which were characterized by a broadly diffused ethos of pluralism. This pluralism (in sentiments, dispositions, etc.) was variably informed by sexual and gendered symbols and practices in ritual domains; by long-term historical dynamics discussed elsewhere (Peletz, forthcoming); and by a nexus of domestic and social structural variables of the sort identified by Beatty (2002) for late-twentieth-century Java (widespread fosterage and adoption, high rates of divorce, terminological usages such as teknonymy, birth-order names, etc.), that give rise to relationality, temporal flux, and reversal, and otherwise encourage conceptual and moral relativism.

The anthropologist Clifford Geertz has recently written that in relation to its counterparts in most other world areas "gender difference" in regions of Southeast Asia such as Java and Bali "is conceived as a derivative, essentially secondary, diffuse, and muted phenomenon" (2006:327; see also Atkinson and Errington 1990; and Peletz 1996, 2006). Ironically, it may be in no small measure because gender has tended to be relatively muted and unmarked in comparison to other, culturally elaborated axes of difference and inequality (e.g., descent, age, birth order, and in recent times social class) that many societies in Southeast Asia have long accommodated and accorded value to degrees and expressions of gender and sexual diversity that have been actualized to a lesser degree (or generally fared less well) elsewhere and as a consequence have helped mark the region as distinctive.

The early modern era, commonly defined as the period stretching roughly from the fifteenth through the eighteenth century, provides clear evidence of gender pluralism in many parts of Southeast Asia. This period in the region's history was characterized by relatively egalitarian relations between males and females, by a good deal of female autonomy and social control, by considerable fluidity and permeability in gender roles, and by relative tolerance and indulgence with respect to things erotic and sexual, at least for the commoner majority (B. Andaya 1994, 2000). Portuguese observers of the sixteenth century reported that Malays were "fond of music and given to love," the broader themes being that "pre-marital sexual relations were regarded indulgently, and [that] virginity at marriage was not expected of either party" (Reid 1988:153). Chinese, Europeans, and others emphasized similar patterns when writing about Thais, Javanese and other Indonesians, Filipinos, and Burmese. They also made it clear that throughout this period women assumed important roles in politics, trade, and diplomacy, and were rarely secluded or veiled, except in the case of elites. Women also predominated in a good many ritual contexts associated with agriculture, birth, death, and healing perhaps because their reproductive capacities were seen as giving them regenerative, spiritual, and other religious powers that men could not match (146).

In light of these patterns, it should not be surprising that throughout the early modern period (and in earlier times as well) many communities of Southeast Asians accorded enormous prestige to male-bodied individuals who dressed in female attire both while performing certain rituals (associated with royal regalia, births, weddings, and the agricultural cycle) and in nonritual, everyday contexts, and who commonly took normatively gendered males as their husbands. These transgendered ritual specialists, along with female-bodied ritualists who sometimes engaged in transgendered behavior and same-sex relations (but appear to have done so in fewer societies than their male-bodied counterparts), served as sacred mediators between males and females, and between the spheres of humans and the domains of spirits and nature.

Much has changed in Southeast Asia since early modern times, as indicated by the discussions of Malays and Singaporeans, but many aspects of the pluralistic ethos of the early modern period remain alive and well. In present-day Thailand, for example, gender-transgressive males known as *kathoeys*, who probably performed important ritual services in royal palaces in times past, are actively involved in spirit mediumship and are typically accorded far more legitimacy and respect than their gender-transgressive counterparts in the West. This despite the fact that they are sometimes derided for behavior that is seen as "unmanly" or "un-Thai." As with the neighboring Khmer/Cambodian variant of *kathoey* (generally rendered either as *kathoey* or *khtoey*), this term appears to have originally referred to hermaphrodites. At present, however, it is most commonly used to designate a male-bodied individual who either walks, talks, or dresses like a woman; spends "too much" time with women; is involved in stereotypically female pastimes or occupations (hairdressing, flower arranging, fashion design); or behaves like a woman in other ways, such as having sex (in the receptor mode) with men (Morris 1994; Jackson 1997).[4]

One of the interesting features of the term and its deployment by Thai speakers is that it does not distinguish among effeminacy, transvestism, transsexualism, and homosexuality. One's erotic orientation toward someone of the same or "opposite" sex, moreover, is not a primary marker of *kathoey*-ness, the more fundamental issue being that the term refers primarily to gender transgression rather than sexual transgression. These generalizations apply to analogous terms in many other Southeast Asian languages, such as the Indonesian *waria* and *banci*, as well as the terms *bakla* and *bantut*, which are utilized in the northern, Christian Philippines and the Muslim south, respectively (see Oetomo 1996; Johnson 1997; and Manalansan 2003). Noteworthy as well is that it is by no means uncommon for a normatively gendered Southeast Asian male to have one or more sexual encounters with a gender-transgressive male (e.g., a *kathoey*, *waria*, *bakla*, or *bantut*) prior to or even during his (heterosexual) marriage. Such an encounter, if made public, does not result in the male losing his claim to normativity or being considered homosexual or *gay*.[5] Nor would it—or an ongoing relationship with such an individual—feminize him, as would typically occur in the West. Conversely, especially in Java and other parts of Indonesia, males who participate in same-sex relations and identify as *gay* tend to be involved in (or plan to enter into) heterosexual marriage leading to procreation, thus fulfilling normative expectations that are in many ways far more weighty than those specifying that sexuality be confined to heterosexual relationships (Boellstorff 1999). In short, as with their counterparts in Thailand, the Philippines, Malaysia, Burma, and Vietnam, these men fashion identities and strategies for survival that entail "drawing variously on endogenous traditions and identities as well as exogenous concepts and practices, combining and recombining them, and at the same time contesting both cultural conventions that would condemn homosexuality as incompatible with filial piety and metropolitan notions that would insist there is only one way to be authentically gay" (Proschan 1998:3).

What then of *tom*s and *dee*s? These terms (and variations such as *T*, *T-bird*, and *tibo*) derive from the English "tomboys" and "ladies", respectively, and are commonly used in Thailand, Indonesia, the Philippines, and elsewhere in Southeast Asia to designate female-bodied individuals who engage in same-sex relations, one or another form of transgenderism, or both. Megan Sinnott (2004), writing on Thailand, has produced the most nuanced and sophisticated anthropological study of *tom*s (masculine females) and *dee*s (feminine females in relationships with masculine females, i.e. *tom*s) to date. Drawing on more than eight years of fieldwork-based research and on scholarly debates in a number of different academic disciplines, Sinnott's study sheds light on the national and global forces that are shaping new gender and sexual identities and senses of self in a rapidly modernizing region of Southeast Asia long regarded by Western travel writers and tourists as a sexual paradise and a haven for gays and lesbians alike.

The emergence in the past few decades of *dee* identities and subjectivities is in many ways most revealing of changes occurring in Thailand and elsewhere in Asia. For what separates *dee*s from normative Thai women is not their gender identities or styles of dress or comportment, all of which are broadly congruent with the contours of Thai femininity, but their sexual orientation, the fact that they are attracted to, desirous of, and erotically involved with women rather than men. What is new and distinctive about these women, in other words, is that their subject positions and subjectivities are defined not only by their female gender but also by their sexual orientation as women who engage in sex with other women. Partly because gender identities in Southeast Asia have always subsumed and effectively defined sexual orientations, scholars such as Dennis Altman (1996, 2001) see in these kinds of developments evidence of the ways in which "Asian homosexualities," to use his terminology, are being "Americanized," "Westernized," or otherwise reconfigured by transnational, globalizing developments (see also Morris 1994).

In my view, however, these shifts are not as dramatic as they may appear at first glance. I say this partly because in Thailand and elsewhere in Southeast Asia feminine-identified *dees* tend to form erotic relationships exclusively with masculine-identified *toms* (in contrast to masculine-identified *gay* men whose sexual relationships do not necessarily involve feminized *gays*). These relationships, though (homo)sexualized, are still heterogender as far as most of the participants and others are concerned. As such, they fit comfortably within the heterogender matrix that has long been a central component of sex/gender systems throughout Southeast Asia. If, on the other hand, the new subject positions involved relationships that were simultaneously homosexual *and* homogender (i.e., of the same sex and similarly or identically gendered), they could pose truly serious challenges to the prevailing hegemony. Note, though, that it would not be the *sexual* patterning—the homosexuality—of these relationships that would raise the specter of subversion vis-à-vis local taxonomies and hierarchies and the values and interests they serve. Rather, the real threat of subversion would come from the way they are *gendered*—the fact that they would be homogender.

Emerging Lesbian Desires and Youth Culture (China)

Material from Thailand and other areas of Southeast Asia is profitably viewed in relation to Tze-Ian D. Sang's *The Emerging Lesbian: Female Same-Sex Desire in Modern China* (2003). This fascinating study of literary and other sources traces the vicissitudes of same-sex desire among Chinese women from late imperial times (especially the eighteenth and nineteenth centuries) through the Republican era (1912–49) and the decades of Maoist rule (1949–78) to the present-day post-Mao period both on the mainland and in neighboring Taiwan. The focus is less on sexual relations per se than on sisterhood and friendship among women, their feelings and fantasies, their "longing[s], physical familiarity, intimacy, commitment, and gender subordination" (42).

In late imperial China (ca. 1600–1911), as in most other parts of Asia during this period, transgender practices and same-sex relations were accorded legitimacy in certain (particularly palace and ritual) contexts, at least if they involved male-bodied individuals. Little is known about women involved in transgender practices or same-sex relations, but it appears that same-sex relations between Chinese women were not so much expressly prohibited (they were not criminalized in traditional legal codes, for example) as denigrated, belittled, or trivialized (Sang 2003:21, 91). Unlike those in the Christian West, however, imperial era Chinese "never expressed . . . a tangible abomination specifically for the sex act between women as unclean, unnatural, a sin, or a crime" (64). What mattered more than a woman's erotic involvement with other women was that she conform to the expectations enjoining her to enter into a legitimate marriage with a man of appropriate genealogy and social standing; that she produce children, especially male heirs, for that man and his patrilineage; and that she remain faithful to him in the sense that she not participate in inappropriate intimacies with other men.

Late imperial representations are

> little concerned with a woman's natural inclinations or fulfillment; rather . . . [they depict] marriage as simply a woman's duty. Women must marry to fulfill their roles as obedient daughters, wives, and mothers. Such obedience to men throughout one's life defines virtuous womanhood, according to Confucian teachings. Therefore, it may be said that *compulsory marriage, compulsory sexual service, compulsory reproduction*, and *compulsory chastity* are more apt than *compulsory heterosexuality* as descriptions of women's fate at the hands of traditional Chinese patriarchy. (Sang 2003:92, emphasis in original)

Elaborating on the theme that during this time "intimacies with women" were ultimately "inconsequential," Sang advances a compelling argument that is relevant far beyond late imperial China and may be a general characteristic across Asia: "What determines a woman's gender conformity or nonconformity is first and foremost her relations with men, not her relations with women. Female-female desire does not render a woman defective or make her a gender outcast as long as it cooperates with the imperative of cross-sex marriage. *In sum, female-female desire by itself is not taboo; marriage resistance is*" (93, emphasis added).

Much of the situation described here changed in the early decades of the twentieth century due to globally far-reaching geopolitical developments, including the spread of European colonialism, print capitalism, and Western scientific discourses, which congealed in a field that came to be known as "sexual science" or "sexology." During the late nineteenth and early twentieth centuries in particular, European and American scientists and scholars such as Sigmund Freud, Carl Jung, Magnus Hirshfeld, Havelock Ellis, Richard von Krafft-Ebing, and Edward Carpenter developed a corpus of scholarship on the anatomy, physiology, genetics, evolution, sociology, and folklore of sexuality that was widely disseminated throughout the world. Much of this scholarship defined transgender practices and same-sex relations as pathological, requiring a cure via medical or psychiatric treatment, although some of the literature promoted more positive views of these phenomena. As elsewhere in the world, the pathological view prevailed. Of broader relevance is the fact that transgender practices, same-sex relations, and what came to be defined as "normal" sex/gender practices and subjectivities were for the first time subject to intense scientific and public scrutiny, having been effectively created as a legitimate object of scientific study and public debate. The military prowess of Western nations in the early twentieth century, when most of Africa, Asia, and the Pacific, and much of the New World as well was subject to Western colonial rule,[6] helped ensure that Western scientific discourses, including sexology, were accorded tremendous prestige throughout the world.

In China, for example, nationalistically oriented intellectuals who sought to break with their feudal past were often inspired by Western models of modernity and progress and thus commonly embraced Western notions of race and evolution, along with attendant concepts of racial hierarchies and racial degeneration, some of which were yoked to sexology. Put differently, "the scientism of Western-oriented May Fourth [early-twentieth-century] intellectuals was assisted by their anxiety over the weakness and regression of the Chinese race, which made them susceptible to the sway of late nineteenth- and early twentieth-century European sexology, which claimed to discover hereditary degeneracy, male effeminacy, and female masculinity in homosexuality" (Sang 2003:16). In China, Japan, and elsewhere in Asia, these developments gave birth to binary notions of sexuality, sexual "essences," and sexual types ("heterosexuality" vs. "homosexuality," "the heterosexual," "the homosexual," etc.) and a host of other Western-origin concepts that had no local counterparts. At the same time, they contributed to the "the sexological abnormalization of same-sex intimacy . . . in many Asian societies" as also occurred "in Europe and America since the early twentieth century" (7).

One of the defining characteristics of the May Fourth era in China was the existence of an intellectual and cultural-political climate conducive to the expression of a wide diversity of views and broad-ranging debates concerning the role and status of women in the family and society at large and whether expressions of their sexuality ought to be limited to the institution of (theoretically) monogamous marriage or could involve pre-and extramarital heterosexual relations and same-sex desire. Unfortunately, this climate of open intellectual exchange did not last long: "[A]s Japanese military aggression escalated in China during the 1930s, growing Chinese nationalism and the leftists' zealous call for socially engaged literature . . . [appear to] have cast an unflattering light on female-female romantic love (as well as heterosexual love), making it seem self-indulgent and irrelevant to the crisis at hand." Similarly, in the wake of Mao Zedong's rise to power and the formation of the People's Republic of China (PRC) in 1949, there occurred a "complete effacement of female same-sex love as a topic for public debate and artistic representation" (Sang 2003:156, 163).

In later years, the Chinese Communist Party (CCP) "harshly denounce[d] homosexuality either as a Western capitalist conception or as a heinous feudalist crime," declaring as well that homosexuality was altogether absent from the PRC (Sang 2003:106, 163). The latter declarations sat uneasily with the public punishment meted out to those suspected of homosexual activity, who were typically charged with "hooliganism" and paraded through the streets carrying signs proclaiming their crimes (167 passim). For the most part, debates about same-sex relations did not reemerge in the public spheres of the PRC until after the Mao's death in 1976 and Deng Xiaoping's 1978 proclamations that the CCP would reassess its commitment to a "purely" socialist path of development and opt for development strategies that entailed an "opening" (*kaifang*) of mainland China to global market forces.

These policy shifts helped set the stage for "the resurgence of liberal feminism in the late 1980s and the 1990s" (Sang 2003:125, 167 passim). They have also had momentous consequences for kinship and gender relations, household dynamics, consumer and "lifestyle" choices, and understandings and experiences of bodies and selves, particularly in rapidly expanding urban areas. Judith Farquhar (2002) describes the situation well. I quote her at length.

> Beginning in the mid 1980s, Chinese modernity began to look a lot more sexy. Several distinct literatures on sex—pornographic novels and magazines, family sexual hygiene manuals, medical sexology, respectable erotic fiction, translations of sexology classics like Havelock's Ellis's *Sexual Psychology* and the Kinsey Report, scholarship in ancient Chinese ars erotica, and a new subdiscipline of traditional medicine called *nanke*, "men's medicine"—emerged and flourished in a book market that was no longer directly controlled by the state. Gender differentiation in the surface of everyday life—dress, cosmetics, and gestural style—became extreme for a while, particularly among the young, with rococo assemblages of ruffles, ribbons, sequins, and satins mostly on women, and leather jackets, cowboy gear, and motorcycle boots mostly on men. In many cities, shops opened where white-coated clerks sell birth-control supplies, condoms, herbal aphrodisiacs, skimpy leather clothing, and sexual aids in a matter-of-fact clinical manner. By the late 1990s, Chinese-made movies had begun to include explicitly filmed sex scenes as a matter of routine. (211)

The proliferation of a number of separate and distinct discourses on sex—some ostensibly "ancient" and "authentically Chinese," others deriving prestige from their association with or definition as "modern science"—has helped fuel the "sexual revolution" in China's urban areas. This is nowhere more apparent than in Shanghai, a megacity of 17 million residents (according to 2006 estimates), which has experienced spectacular economic growth, with income quadrupaling over the last decade and "GDP growth rates over 14 percent in the mid-1990s" (Farrer 2002:4). James Farrer's (2002) sociological study of youth sex culture and market reform in Shanghai documents the far-ranging effects of what many in China speak of as *kaifang*. This term, which means "opening" or "opening up," refers to China's increased responsiveness and greater vulnerability to both global capitalism and the attendant temptations and seductions of Western-style consumer culture, including the cult of the materialistic, pleasure-seeking, narcissistic individual that consumer cultures both target and create. For people in Shanghai, especially youth, this trajectory has brought radically increased living standards and unprecedented personal freedom and choice in the realms of dating, leisure, and consumption, although many in Shanghai and elsewhere would say too much freedom and too many choices.

Developments in Shanghai and other parts of China in the past few decades have simultaneously given rise to a critical range of uncertainties, insecurities, and ambivalences as well, as has also occurred in socialist Vietnam since the onset of Doi Moi (Renovation) in 1986 (Pelzer 1993). Particularly in China, some of the most unsettling insecurities are material. As capitalist market forces, premised on a logic of supply and demand, replace or supersede centralized state control over production, distribution, and consumption, and therefore employment opportunities, young Chinese no longer enjoy the job or overall economic security they once did. Overcrowded and ever more congested urban areas, coupled with the scarcity and expense of urban housing and the premium placed on geographic and social mobility geared toward the attainment of "success" (which guarantees continued migration from rural to urban locales), all contribute to the undermining of extended family ties, hence the erosion of networks of social security to which one could formerly turn in times of economic need. New and old rationales for gender discrimination in wages, promotions, work conditions, and employment opportunities exacerbate the situation for women. Circumstances such as these encourage women to view dance hall encounters and dating as an opportunity to improve their short- and long-term material standing, just as they give rise to discourses on "greedy Shanghai girls" obsessed with fashion and appearance and the "weak Shanghai men" who succumb to their superficial—if only because ephemeral and easily transferable—"charms" (affections, loyalties, sexual services).

One indication of the incredibly rapid transformation of Shanghai's commercial and cultural landscapes is the twenty-five-fold increase that occurred from the mid-1980s to the mid-1990s in the number of commercial dance halls (discos). Discos numbered a mere 52 in 1985 and an astounding (if only in comparative terms) 1,347 in 1996 (Farrer 2002:291)! The spread of disco culture helped "normalize —actually glorified—sexual voyeurism and display. Young women who would have been careful not to show themselves as 'loose' in daily life could dance with wild pelvic thrusts or snuggle up to a stranger in a slow two-step" and "[a]ll could [later] be forgotten as a passing silliness" or "just fooling around" (301). "Mistrust was the ideology of the dance, but curious interaction was the practice," especially since for some patrons, who were mostly students, "it was a chance to find casual sexual partners" (305). Interestingly, while many of the icons of chic in the early years of the disco scene hailed from America, by 1999 Japan had superseded America as the preeminent source of fashion (though American styles were still to be found, along with those from Hong Kong and Korea). Farrer notes, for example, that in 1999 "the youth at Buff [a popular Shanghai disco] . . . sported fashion elements that I recognized immediately from the pages of Japanese style manuals that I saw youth perusing in Shanghai: punky orange hair, platform boots, little black party dresses, pigtails shooting out sideways under cute knit hats, the stocking caps of Tokyo rappers, thick-rimmed glasses, and glitter eye shadow." By the following year, however, Japanese and other "foreigners were no longer the models of style and behavior they used to be," having been replaced by locals (311, 322).

The sexual revolution that has occurred most dramatically in Shanghai, and to a lesser extent in other urban areas of China, clearly has a downside, including a "surge in divorce, premarital sex, extramarital affairs, . . . new type[s] of financially motivated pragmatism in marriage," and the "reemergence of concubinage" and polygyny among the wealthy (Farrer 2002:133, 144). The 1990s also saw a sharp rise in rates of sexually transmitted diseases in Shanghai: "273 percent for herpes" and "122 percent for syphilis." National-level data likewise revealed startling increases in reports of STDs, which grew from "1,000 per year in 1983 to over 300,000 per year in 1994 . . . Most men were contracting STDs from commercial sex, while women were likely contracting STDs from their regular partners who visited prostitutes" (359–60 n. 15).

Not surprisingly, the scarring via STDs of bodies, relationships, psyches, and senses of self that has occurred due to market reform and globalization has gone hand in hand with the development of a widespread cynicism about "the possibility of romance" and the "purity of purpose or motive" (Farrer 2002:224 passim). Women often suspect the behavior of men due to men's media-hyped desire to appear to be "playboys" or "(cool) players" in games of sexual conquest (discussed in more detail below). Men, for their part, are often suspicious of the comportment of women for reasons noted earlier: because "at heart, they're all 'gold diggers'" and because virginity, which is still highly valued in a potential wife, is an increasingly uncommon attribute of young women. As laden with ambivalence as they are, such are the "facts of life" in a consumer culture that engenders heavy anxiety about performance in the rough and tumble of bedroom, boardroom, and back alley.

Contexts such as these gave rise to and help explain the enormous popularity in the Chinese-speaking world, and in East Asia and the Chinese diaspora generally, of film stars such as Bruce Lee, Jackie Chan, and Chow Yun Fat. These megastars, along with the martial arts, action films, and video games with which they are iconically associated, offer compelling alternatives to the discourses on "weak, effeminate Chinese men" that have circulated in Shanghai and elsewhere at various points in the twentieth century and earlier times. The latter discourses repeatedly singled out "the crisis of (Chinese) masculinity" as the primary cause of China's poor showing, both politically and economically, on the modern world stage. China's early- to mid twentieth-century reputation in the West as "the sick man of Asia," which is "still bitterly remembered today" (Louie 2002:101), is clearly relevant in this context. The films and other media products at issue here engage Hollywood constructions of masculinity. But they also glorify the cultivation of self-control and refinement through martial arts and other regimes of discipline that promote physical strength, military prowess, homosocial bonding, and heterosexual abstinence or at least careful regulation of sexual and emotionally deep relations with women. These themes resonate with Confucian and other Chinese ethics emphasizing that control of the self is a prerequisite for rising to positions of power and prestige that involve control over others. It is revealing in this connection that "in the 1990s, immensely popular television soap operas such as *Beijingers in New York* and *Foreign Babes in Beijing* unambiguously correlated sexual 'conquest' of white women with national revival, so that: 'The victory that Chinese men are able to score with foreign women symbolizes not only the resurrection of Chinese masculinity but also a triumph of the Chinese nation itself'" (Lu 2000, cited in Louie 2002:75).

Sexual Politics and Popular Culture (Taiwan and Japan)

The historical development and contemporary contours of youth culture in Shanghai cannot be taken as typifying mainland China let alone the Greater China that includes the numerous and far-flung residents of the diaspora. That said, analogous phenomena have been reported for other large cities of

China and may well be a harbinger of national trends. This seems all the more likely in light of China's intense drive to industrialize its economy, eliminate rural poverty, and create a largely urban workforce. Developments in popular culture and sexual politics on the other side of the Taiwan Strait are relevant here inasmuch as they suggest one of several possible futures that might unfold on the mainland. In any event, they merit consideration in their own right. So, too, in different ways, do comparisons involving popular culture and sexual politics in Taiwan and Japan, each of which has embraced capitalist development with a vengeance and has developed its own distinct vision of modernity.

Many of the sexual and gender dynamics occurring in Shanghai and other highly urban areas of China in recent years bear a close resemblance to developments in Taiwan over the past few decades. Major differences also exist due to historical and geopolitical factors whose influence continues to be strongly felt. Unlike the situation in China, for example, American political and military institutions played a key role in Taiwan's development for over fifty years (since 1949 when Gen. Chiang Kai-shek suffered defeat at the hands of Mao's revolutionary forces, fled the mainland of China with his Kuomintang army, and, with massive American assistance, set up headquarters and a government across the strait in Taiwan). From the outset, Taiwan's American-backed military rulers and the institutions through which they governed embodied and disseminated a broad range of beliefs and practices associated with American capitalism and Western culture in general, although they did not give priority to American-style democracy. Due to political repression under martial law, which prevailed through 1987, opposition movements of various stripes developed, many of which drew inspiration from American writings on freedom, justice, and equality. American cultural influences are also much in evidence on university campuses (among students and academics alike), in intellectual circles beyond academia, in journalism and other mass media, in the arts, in feminist movements, and in the realms of lesbian and gay activism. This is not to suggest that such influences have erased or supplanted the role of Chinese culture in these or other areas. It is, rather, a relative point, underscoring differences between Taiwan and mainland China, where such influences are far less evident (Sang 2003).

In Taiwan, as in many parts of the world, popular culture is influenced and in some respects created by an increasingly internationalized media driven by a combination of homegrown and transnational corporate capitalisms. The media in Taiwan seek to capture the hearts and minds both of consumers charged with household provisioning and "status production work," who, as we have seen in our discussions of Korea and Singapore, are generally women, and of others in various "niche markets." Here, too, feminism sells, as does the marshaling via television talk shows and other media outlets of popular opinion arrayed against it. So, too, increasingly, do media and commercial products that target the burgeoning lesbian and gay subcultures that exist in Taiwan and Hong Kong but not yet on any comparable scale elsewhere in China. Mass media in particular might give the impression of a comfortable or mutually supportive relationship in Taiwan between feminism and lesbian (and gay) activism, but "in actual political practice, even feminists in the most radical women's organization have questioned the legitimacy of lesbian agendas in the women's movement" (Sang 2003:237). Lesbians tend to find their concerns marginalized or ignored by the women's movement, though the situation may be changing. Further complicating the prospects for cooperation is the fact that "some lesbians (esp. Ts [tomboys or butches]) resist female identity," having "always fought against" what they take to be "the institutional violence of heterosexuality." Hence they experience difficulties embracing one of the most basic principles of feminism: that "women identify with women" (242).

In her incisive discussion of mass media and the commercialization of homosexuality, Tze-Ian Sang notes that Taiwanese, like people in most countries, receive the bulk of their knowledge about the world from the media, and that media organizations such as Taiwan's, while generally conservative, present consumers with coverage of Western events that is often relatively positive, though simultaneously sensationalistic, voyeuristic, and shot full of negative stereotypes. These generalizations are highly germane to the coverage afforded dynamics of sexual culture in America, especially "gay pride" parades, the ravages and scope of the AIDS epidemic, the development of AIDS activism, gay and lesbian marriage, and various aspects of same-sex sexuality. In treating these topics and their Taiwanese counterparts, the media, particularly the tabloids, endeavor to titillate and shock their audiences with dramas of sexual escapades and criminality via "story after story about lesbian/gay promiscuity, sexual techniques, cruising parks and bars, crimes, murders, and suicides." Sang (2003:247) characterizes some of these accounts as "voyeuristic," others as "plainly fantastic."

The media's excitement over their "discovery" of lesbians in the early 1990s raises some potentially unsettling questions that are also worth raising in other contexts, including that of the United States: "If homosexuality has become one of the most trendy and best-selling topics in Taiwan, is it because lesbians and gays have become such a distinctive and powerful consumer group that their emotional needs and erotic interests must be catered to?" Or does the recent development of "lesbian/gay chic" reflect the fact that "lesbian/gay sexualities have been domesticated and turned into curiosities that an audience that considers itself normal will find entertaining?" (Sang 2003:248–49).

From Sang's perspective, the dynamic suggested by each of these questions helps explain current trends in media and popular culture in Taiwan, as does the fact that openly gay media tend to embrace consumerism and many of the underlying values (individualism, materialism, etc.) it reinforces.

In Taiwan, the Internet has become not only an integral component of the commercialization and mass mediation of same-sex sexuality but also a powerful technology deployed to resist commercialization and mass mediation as well as the panoply of forces that seek to silence local gay and lesbian voices. One of the signature features of the Internet is the near instantaneous global connectedness it provides its users. In Taiwan, as elsewhere, the Internet has made locally available information concerning Western sexual cultures, as is true to a lesser extent of other media: "The rise in Taiwan during the last decade of novels and whole collections dealing with the subject of lesbian eroticism and lesbian subjectivity . . . occurred amid a burgeoning lesbian and gay identity politics and the general proliferation of queer discourses" that "swept through the island during the early to mid-1990s" (Sang 2003:256, 258). Just as some local academic critics "tirelessly cite Western queer theory," certain "local queer theorists are so popular with readers and audiences that they have become media celebrities." Deeply ambivalent about such developments, Sang contends that an "uncritical parroting of the latest trends in First World queer theory" is "quite the opposite of being queer. Worse still, it might mean misdirecting valuable resources away from, rather than toward, the really challenging problems of local sexual and gender politics" (258, 260, 261).

More important in the larger scheme of things, "the Internet has emerged as a powerful new public medium and forum. It has proved remarkably effective in supporting non-profit feminist and antihomophobic publishing as well as open, well-circulated discussion under relatively safe and anonymous conditions. Such decentralization of mass communication greatly contributes to the proliferation of lifestyles, and vice versa" (Sang 2003:231). Concerning the future, Sang speculates, "If the Internet continues to maintain its autonomy, radical movements in Taiwan such as lesbian activism and feminism are likely increasingly to employ it for carving out and maintaining a critical public sphere. We have reason to hope that, as opinions become contested and liberalized in cyberspace, transformations in this emerging domain of the cultural imaginary will catalyze changes in the material conditions of the so-called reality as well" (254).

Despite the heightened visibility of lesbian and gay communities in recent years, Taiwanese society as a whole by no means embraces either lesbians or gay men. In addition to having to battle the powerful but conservative media that simultaneously stereotypes them but also uses them as marketing tools to "pry into and capitalize on the eroticism of a formative urban lesbian scene," lesbians in particular must contend with "the Confucian patriarchal family transfigured by the influence of the modern nuclear family [which] continues to prescribe and privilege a particular alignment between biological sex, culturally defined gender behavior, and romantic/erotic desire" (Sang 2003:228, 232). Bolstered and legitimized by a conservative medical profession, "this regime of gender and sexuality dictates that, to be considered normal, a woman [must] accept a male spouse, join his family, and fulfill her reproductive destiny." As in mainland China, Singapore, and elsewhere, "the modern heterosexual regime works against women's same-sex desire, not only by denouncing and prohibiting it, but also by silencing it, erasing it, rendering it unthinkable, invisible, and insignificant," just as the "typical family," when forced to react, moves to "reject . . . punish . . . or 'fix'" the errant female (232).

While Taiwan's lesbian movement is more developed and "robust" than its counterparts in other Chinese-speaking societies (in mainland China, Hong Kong, and Singapore, for instance), it differs in significant ways from the local movement centered around gay men, a contrast that also exists in other Chinese-speaking contexts and, indeed, in much of the world. One of the most revealing differences is that lesbians in Taiwan cannot readily draw upon a historical past to help provide legitimacy for their practices and identities, even though scholars have documented scattered (apparently regionally specific) traditions of marriage resistance and female same-sex sexuality that existed in Greater China in earlier times (see, e.g., Sankar 1986). The relative absence, except in literary contexts, of such traditions helps clarify two sets of issues. The first has to do with why discourses of Western origin have been of such importance in Taiwan and in many other parts of Asia throughout the twentieth century and into the new millennium. The second concerns why, despite terms of indigenous origin such as *tongzhi* (comrade, cadre), which was appropriated from the Maoist period and is utilized in Hong Kong and the PRC, many of the terms utilized by Taiwanese and other Asian women attracted to women involve borrowings from the West, for instance, *tomboy* and *t* (short for *tomboy*). Gay men, in contrast, can—and do—point to well-known historical traditions that involved male-male sexuality (such as those that existed in imperial circles, for example) as a way to both legitimize their subject positions and subjectivities and to counter state-sanctioned ideologies that portray them as unacceptable local parodies of Western perversion. As Sang (2003:54) puts it, albeit somewhat dismissively for the males to whom she refers, "The sense of not having a usable Chinese past distinguishes the experience of many ethnic Chinese lesbians from that of the many gay men who cling to the fantasy of belonging to a great homosexual tradition in China."

A proliferation of sexual subcultures has also occurred in Japan, where non-normative sex sells and sells big. This is partly because since the early decades of the twentieth century state-sponsored corporate capitalists have conjured all varieties of erotic imagery in the service of creating and aggressively marketing a broad range of media products aimed at titillating, seducing, and otherwise captivating customers and thus giving rise to and (ideally) capturing increasingly lucrative market shares. At present, such imagery includes depictions of scantily clad teenage girls and women, cross-dressing actors, and androgynous "She-Male" figures who abound "in ordinary and pornographic comic books alike, . . . [in] fantastical, exotic, intersexed, androgynous bodies, most typically portrayed in the form of a figure with breasts and a penis" (Robertson 1998:201). The term "New Half" (*nyu hafu*) is sometimes used to refer to these comics, as well as the members of the youth subcultures who consume them, including, most notably, the growing numbers of males who in niche clubs and other contexts attire themselves in female clothing, emulating the "fictive men (in comic books, for example) who cross-dress in the much fetishized style of Lolitas, or sexually precocious, cute teenage girls" (2001). As the anthropologist Jennifer Robertson, an expert on Japanese sexuality, explains, the root term "half" (*hafu*) is often used as a derogatory term to refer to locals of ethnically mixed parentage, and the designation New Half thus reflects the Japanese sense that gender and sexual ambiguity entail ethnic (or "racial") ambiguity and vice versa.

The mutually constitutive nature of these ambiguities—and of the ambivalences associated with them—is clear from the history of Japan's famous Takarazuka Revue, the brainchild of legendary Japanese venture capitalist and cabinet minister Kobayashi Ichizo (1873–1957). The all-female members of this theatrical troupe, which was founded in 1913, frequently engage in both cross-dressing and "cross-ethnicking"—portraying members of other ethnic groups, particularly those colonized by Japan during World War II—and thus constitute "exoticized hybrids" par excellence (Robertson 1998:201). The Revue, though both innovative and more or less acceptably transgressive, builds on earlier traditions of gender and sexuality in Japan, including those that prevailed during the Tokugawa period (1603–1867), during which time bisexuality tended to be the norm for males (but not females) and male homoeroticism was privileged over eroticism of all other varieties, much as in ancient Greece (Louie 2002:24; cf. Pflugfelder 1999:5 passim). Ironically, the erotics and cultural politics of the Revue are simultaneously informed by the ethos of the Meiji Restoration (dating from 1868), which gave rise to a greater formalization of gender roles in line with increasingly Western-inflected and dichotomized understandings of gender and sexuality, including the imposition of new and more restrictive legal codes premised on the idea that ambiguity involving gender and sexuality is conducive to widely redounding social disorder. Thus targeted was cross-dressing on the part of males in Kabuki performances along with much of the homoeroticism and same-sex sexuality that prevailed among samurai during the preceding Tokugawa period, as famously (and scandalously) depicted in Nagisa Oshina's 1999 film *Gohatto* (glossed as *Taboo* in English-speaking venues), which has become something of a cult classic among contemporary Japanese males involved in same-sex relations.

Referring to the "recent fascination in Japanese popular culture with androgyny and cross-dressing" Robertson makes clear that "androgyny is big business. New Half comic books and animations, transvestite clubs for males, Miss Dandy clubs for females, clothing fashions, cross-dressed celebrities, and of course the perennially popular Takarazuka Revue, enjoying an all-time high number of applicants to the academy, are all part of the powerful and metaphoric—if ambivalent—salience of androgyny" (1998:205). So, too, are the comic books aimed at women that "specialize in the homoerotic adventures of *bishonen* or 'beautiful boys' . . . whose forbidden and often tragic love . . . is [seen as] somehow more 'pure' and more 'equal' than that which exists between men and women, constrained as they are by the reproductive demands of the family system" (McLelland 2002:7).

Also relevant in this context is Gao, "a Japanese version of the gender-bending Canadian popular singer k.d. lang. The Japanese pop icon was discovered —or rather, invented—in 1993. Her public relations campaign capitalizes on and commodifies the image of the androgyne" as is evident from some of the English-language publicity statements aimed at Japanese consumers: "How does Gao spend her one-day-of-the-year? That voice, that prescence, that style -- A man? Or is it a woman? How old is she? What's her true sexuality? A million possibilities surface, but if we look at her, none seem to fit. She's unlike anyone else. She's Gao!" (cited in Robertson 1998:205). It is important to bear in mind that Gao's persona is "the creation not of some radical queer underground but of a powerful corporation (in this case, Victor Entertainment)," much like the Takarazuka Revue, "a component of the giant Hankyu Group of companies" (207).

As might be expected, the aggressive marketing in Japan of things sexual and the extensive flows throughout Japan of increasingly global discourses on sex, gender, and romance have given rise to the inclusion in everyday spoken Japanese of English-origin loanwords such as "gay pride" (*gei puraido*), "coming out" (*kamingu auto*), "homophobia" (*homofobia*), and the like. One should not assume, however, that Western and other global influences in Japan are evident only in arenas of gender and sexuality that are to one or another degree marginal with respect to "mainstream" (normative) Japanese

66

culture. Much as we have seen in Korea, Christian, Western-style weddings for heterosexual couples now predominate in Japan, with some three-quarters of all weddings involving quintessentially Western attire, ministers, and music such as "Ave Maria," despite the fact that less than 2 percent of Japan's population of 127 million people is Christian (Brooke 2005). Traditional Shinto marriage ceremonies have lost favor due to their association with what are increasingly seen as conservative gender roles, just as Christian, Western-style weddings offered by corporate bridal companies are all the rage both on grounds of fashion and because of the greater degree of equality between husband and wife and the relative autonomy of the bridal couple vis-à-vis encompassing networks of kin (both "blood" and affinal) that they are taken to symbolize. Some elders see much cause for alarm in these and related trends involving a rejection of long-sanctified tradition, particularly since they are occurring in a climate characterized by falling birthrates, a rise in divorce, and growing cultural emphases on individualism, materialism, and immediate gratification. The larger issue for many in Asia is what current trends portend for the future.

4

Bodies on the Line

As in the rest of the world, many people in Asia view the dawn of the new millennium with mixed feelings, hopeful but far from convinced that urbanization, industrialization, and other processes of modernization will bring a better tomorrow. There are experiential grounds for guarded optimism that developments in science, technology, and political economic arenas will facilitate additional advances in realms that have already seen significant improvement. It is widely assumed, for example, that the years to come will witness increased rates of literacy, further reductions of infant mortality, the decline and eventual elimination of largely preventable diseases, and longer life expectancy. People in many quarters also expect that the future will bring the spread of meaningful democracy that involves not only fair and open elections but also the institutionalization of forms of state, family, and civil society that encourage the fluorescence of sentiments and dispositions conducive to the expansion of civic pluralism, social justice, and equality.

There is, at the same time, considerable cause for concern, especially if, as seems quite likely, the twentieth century is any indication of future trends. The twentieth century saw great strides forward in many areas, but it also witnessed the latest developments in science, technology, and bureaucratic administration being harnessed to the pursuit of devastating warfare and genocidal annihilation. The total number of fatalities (both military and civilian) in World War I (1914–18) and World War II (1939–45), for instance, surpassed 60 to 70 million.[1] American-led wars in Korea (1950–53) and Vietnam (1950–75) resulted in the loss of approximately 100,000 American lives and the deaths of some 2.8 to 3.0 million Koreans and 1 to 3 million Vietnamese. Maoist programs in China during 1949–75 may have caused the demise of as many as 40 million Chinese. And Pol Pot's brief reign of terror in Cambodia during 1975–79 led to the deaths of 1.7 to 2.1 million people, over 20 percent of that country's entire population. To this must be added the genocidal policies that Turks pursued against the Armenians from 1915 to 1918, which resulted in 1.0 to 1.5 million Armenian fatalities, and the World War II Holocaust engineered by National Socialist (Nazi) Germany against Jews, as well as Romany (Gypsies), homosexuals, and others, which claimed the lives of over 6 million people.

There is no need to expand this grim list to underscore that processes of modernity are not all progress and purification or freedom, liberation, and enlightenment. There is a dark side to these processes, involving scales of violence and terror unimaginable in times past as well as the proliferation of technologies of discipline, surveillance, and control that have long alarmed philosophers, social scientists, and others in all walks of life. As students and scholars concerned with understanding how modernity in Asia or elsewhere is experienced, understood, and represented, we need to deal seriously with these dynamics. For this reason, I devote the penultimate section of this booklet to a consideration of modern contexts in which Asian bodies are very much "on the line," particularly as a consequence of the spread of militarization, global tourism, prostitution, AIDS, and "fundamentalism." I conclude with a discussion of social activism in an age of global connection, which provides more positive perspectives on the recent past as well as the present and future.

Militarization, Global Tourism, Prostitution, AIDS (Thailand, the Philippines, and Beyond)

The Cold War which pitted the United States and Western European nations against the USSR and mainland China entailed militarization in many parts of the world and a number of American-led wars on Asian soil (in Korea, Vietnam, and the rest of former French Indochina, for example). These wars helped set the stage for the development of global tourist industries, which appear to have forever changed the face of Asian countries such as Korea, Vietnam, the Philippines, and, most notably, Thailand, the focus of my remarks here.

As a result of official agreements established between the strongly anticommunist governments of Thailand and the United States during the mid-1960s, Thailand served as the main "rest and recreation" headquarters for American and other Allied troops during the war in Vietnam, a war that also involved Cambodia and Laos, hence all of Indochina. Precise figures for the overall number of American and other Allied troops that were stationed in or around Indochina during the war are difficult to come by, but their numbers were probably around 2.5 to 3.0 million, many of whom visited Thailand on multiple occasions during the 1960s and early to mid-1970s. Overwhelmingly male and mostly heterosexual, these troops were encouraged both by their superiors and by their childhood and adult socialization as males to believe that one of the perquisites of military service was "good, clean fun." This fun commonly involved the consumption of large quantities of liquor (and, for some, marijuana and other drugs), as well as all varieties of cheap sex with "exotic," "sensuous," and deeply compliant "oriental" girls and women whose only expectation in return for sexual favors and the appearance of emotional attentiveness and affection seemed to be the equivalent of a few U.S. dollars. The mechanics and cultural politics of war thus created not just a huge demand for Thai (and other Asian) sex workers but also enormously complex transnational industries centered around sex, "hospitality," and entertainment that cater to foreign desires.

The end of America's war in Vietnam and Indochina in 1975 did not bring about the demise of these industries, especially since large numbers of American servicemen are still stationed in or offshore Thailand, Singapore, the Philippines, and elsewhere in Southeast Asia and surrounding areas in accordance with America's "Pacific Rim security strategy" and the Bush administration's "war on terror." On the contrary, the end of the war saw the reorganization, rationalization, and expansion of these industries in response to the development in the 1980s and 1990s of global tourism and sex tourism in particular. Tourism industries generating billions of dollars each year have marketed Bangkok and southern Thai beach resorts such as Pattaya and Phuket as the world's most enticing locales, literal "sexual Disneylands", for both the lone(ly) male traveler and groups of males seeking sex and affection (ostensibly unlike what is available at home) who sign up for package sex tours originating in the United States, Europe, and Australia, as well as Japan, Korea, China, Taiwan, the Middle East, and elsewhere.

These dynamics created much of the demand for Thai sex workers and the Burmese, Laotian, southern Chinese, and former hill-dwelling ethnic minorities who toil in Thailand's sex industry, often against their will, although it should be noted that many Thai men also engage the services of prostitutes. As for the supply side of the equation and the rough numbers of girls and women directly involved in providing sex for cash, the number of sex workers in Thailand has proven difficult to estimate. There are at least two reasons for this. First, although prostitution is condoned and encouraged by government policies, members of the police, military, and border guards, and international business and financial institutions (including upscale international hotel chains), which greatly facilitate sex tourism, it is officially illegal. And, second, the range and sheer number of venues that offer women and girls (as well as boys of all ages)—from brothels, beer halls, disco clubs, five-star hotels, and massage parlors to hair and manicure salons, coffee shops, restaurants, and video rental shops—is extensive. Estimates of the number of girls and women directly involved in commercial sex work commonly range from 200,000 to 300,000 at the lower end of the continuum to 1 to 2 million at the upper end, with the latter figure probably being the more realistic.[2]

The work conditions and health of women and girls involved in the sex industry tend to be grim, especially since their bodies are commodities over which they have very little control. For the majority who work in brothels, bars, beer halls, disco clubs, and similar venues, work conditions are dictated by "management"—club owners, pimps, "mamasans," and the entertainment and black market cartels, which are often linked to the police, the military, or powerful government figures, whose members call the shots. Management often feeds and houses the women and advances them (or their parents) the money necessary to pay their travel expenses from their natal communities (typically "upcountry") to Bangkok and help reduce rural debt. Squalid and cramped living conditions lacking proper sanitation contribute to high rates of illness (respiratory diseases, intestinal disorders), as does Bangkok's notorious air pollution. The repetitive and arduous labor involved in servicing multiple customers every evening, six or seven days a week, contributes to sores and infections, including of course STDs such as HIV/AIDS. In the late 1980s, the Thai government belatedly recognized HIV/AIDS as both a grave health problem and a looming disaster for public relations, tourism, and foreign exchange. 2005/2006 estimates suggest that there are nearly 600,000 cases of HIV/AIDS in Thailand and that the vast majority were contracted via heterosexual prostitution (either directly or indirectly, as when a man who has contracted the virus from a prostitute proceeds to infect his wife).[3] The percentage of sex workers infected with the virus is at least 10 percent but could be much higher. Not all prostitutes are tested regularly, and those who do test positive often try to conceal the results and their declining health in order to keep management in the dark and thus retain their livelihoods.

Growing awareness throughout Thailand and beyond of the large numbers of local prostitutes infected with HIV/AIDS has fueled the demand for ever "younger" (read uninfected) girls, especially virgins. Labor recruiters troll rural communities and border areas populated by Burmese refugees, among others, looking for teenage and prepubescent girls (and boys), just as they range beyond Thailand's borders into Burma, Laos, and Cambodia, for example. They typically promise legitimate employment opportunities to unsuspecting families stricken with economic debt and other rural hardships who might be willing to send a daughter to the capital for a job promising an attractive income with the possibility of high rates of remittance to parents. In mostly agrarian Thailand, farmers commonly lack access to proper irrigation facilities, affordable loans, and cheap credit, largely as a result of state development priorities and policies of international financial institutions such as the World Bank and the International Monetary Fund (Bishop and Robinson 1998). Rural debt, moreover, is often crushing, and employment outside the agrarian sector tends to be limited to tourism, entertainment, and prostitution in particular. Hence there are few other viable options for daughters to make a living and earn cash for remittance to their parents. It is significant that a desire to help parents escape the clutches of poverty is one of the main factors motivating Thai girls and young women to join the ranks of sex workers. In short, concerns with filial piety of the same general sort that motivate women to engage in factory work in Korea, Japan, Taiwan, Malaysia, Singapore, Indonesia, and elsewhere in Asia are commonly cited by Thai prostitutes as one of their primary rationales for working in the skin trade.

Thailand is distinctive in the Asian context inasmuch as its stunning economic transformation has been fueled primarily by revenue from tourism, as distinct from the manufacturing sector that generated the capital surpluses conducive to economic booms elsewhere in Asia. Nevertheless, female labor in the latter industry, specifically the labor of perhaps as many as two million commercial sex workers, has provided most of the earnings generated within Thailand's tourist industry. In sum, in Thailand, too, female labor has underwritten an "economic miracle."

The Philippines, an American colony from 1898 to 1946 and a staunch ally and steadfast supplier of labor and mail-order brides (some would say a neocolony) ever since, is another Asian country in which a huge U.S. military presence fueled the growth of an enormous sex industry with many of the same problems seen in Thailand. This is one reason why, beginning in the 1970s and 1980s, Filipino feminists began impressing upon the public that U.S. policies entailing the militarization of the Philippines were very much a "women's issue" (Enloe 1990:86). The extent to which the U.S. military presence has dominated the economic and cultural political environments of the Philippines has been examined by Cynthia Enloe, a pioneer in feminist analyses of international politics. Referring to the relationship between the Subic Bay Naval Base, which remained open through 1992, and the nearest town (Olongapo City), Enloe observed in the late 1980s that "the Navy base is home for many of the 15,000 American military personnel and their families stationed in the Philippines" and that "when an aircraft-carrier docks, another 18,000 men pour into town" seeking many of the same kinds of "hospitality" and "entertainment" retailed in Bangkok. More generally, "By 1985 the US military had become the second largest employer in the Philippines, hiring over 40,000 Filipinos: 20,581 full-time workers, 14,249 contract workers, 5,064 domestics, and 1,764 concessionaries." "Entertainment workers," mostly female, were estimated in 1987 to number as many as 20,000, although "another 5,000 women often come to Olongapo City from Pampanga Province and Manila when one of the American aircraft-carriers comes into port" (86–87). Perhaps most disturbing is the brisk traffic in children, a problem of immense proportions as well in both Thailand and neighboring Burma: "In recent years rising numbers of [Filipino] children have been recruited into the prostitution trade. Of the approximately 30,000 children born each year of Filipino mothers and American fathers, some 10,000 are thought to become street children, many of them working as prostitutes servicing American pedophiles" (87; cf. Altman 2001:146–7).[4]

Fieldwork conducted in the early 1990s among sex workers in Cebu City, which has a population of over a million people and is thus the second-largest city in the Philippines, reveals analogous patterns. These include double-digit unemployment (aggravated by double-digit underemployment) and a thriving skin trade where "More than half of ... [the] sex industry workers are employed in karaoke bars, bikini bars, and massage parlors, ... establishments [that] are most frequently visited by tourists" (Law 1997:240). The narratives of women involved in the industry, many of whom "perceive their employment as encompassing a variety of functions, including tour guide, interpreter, girlfriend, and prospective wife" (241), are instructive, revealing as they do the ways women move among different employment opportunities, variously defined relationships with men, and diverse arenas in which they might gain locally valued experience and respect. One prostitute, when asked whether her female coworkers might take another job if the opportunity presented itself, responded:

> Why should she go back to the hard life? She's already been there, that's why she's in the [karaoke or bikini] bar. Why be a martyr? Working in a bar is OK if you work hard. It makes you smarter. If a woman has low education, like grades 3 or 4, then if she works in a bar she becomes smarter. She gets to meet professional men, go to expensive restaurants, more than even a teacher can. She has more chances to experience and learn. Me, I'm just like this, but I've met the owners of the big hotels here, and we've been talking. Sometimes I say to myself, if I was staying in my province, I would not meet the owner of the S. hotel. He knows where I come from ... My friend, she's only grade 4, but she learned English and became more confidant. She's got a new hairstyle, some new clothes, and people started calling her ma'am. She dresses in white and goes to the casino. When people ask her what she's doing on the jeepney, she says she's working the night shift at Chong Hua Hospital. (243).

Noteworthy here is the fact that prostitution is depicted, and apparently experienced, as a "choice." That said, it is a choice exercised in an impoverished environment where women (and men) lack educational opportunities and meaningful employment alternatives and the Catholic church promotes ideologies of gender that characterize "[n]onvirgins and single mothers ... [as]

74

'loose' and therefore unmarriageable," thus encouraging their participation in the few remunerative endeavors available to them (245).

Researchers, journalists, and others familiar with the lives and experiences of sex workers have consistently reported that Western men commonly expect Filipino, Thai, and other Asian women to be "not only physically beautiful and sexually exciting but also caring, compliant, submissive, and not 'Western' or 'modern'" (Manderson 1995:309 cited in Law 1997:246). Partly for this reason, Siriporn Skrobanek, of Thailand's Foundation of Women, has suggested:

> Perhaps the most effective way to reduce sex tourism would be to make Thai prostitutes more professional, more like their counterparts in the West, so that they perform their job more mechanistically, without any frills or feelings, with no display of emotion. They should also become more expensive. Then it will stop. Men will stop coming if they find the sex workers here have the same attitude as those in their own countries and charge the same high prices. (Cited in Seabrook 2001:144).

There are, in any event, "more women [in the Philippines] working as prostitutes in the tourist industry than around US bases" (Enloe 1990:87), and the same is true of Thailand. This is largely because "distorted investment, patriarchal conventions and short-sighted government priorities have together forced thousands of poor women off the land and out of exploitative jobs to service civilian as well as military men." That said, twenty-two of the initial twenty-five cases of HIV that had been reported in the Philippines by 1987 were found among women who worked as "entertainers" in the bars around U.S. military bases (87, 88). Since that time, AIDS has became a far more serious problem in the Philippines (and among Filipinos overseas). The most reliable estimates indicate that in 2005 there were approximately twelve thousand people in the Philippines with HIV/AIDS. This figure is relatively low for a country with a population of nearly ninety million people. However, it is quite likely to increase exponentially as a consequence of political and economic dynamics fueling the burgeoning sex industry and the Catholic church's unwavering refusal to countenance the use of condoms, even, or especially, among sex workers and their clients and husbands and wives.

Thailand and the Philippines are certainly not the only countries in Asia suffering from an AIDS epidemic. Indeed, the ravages of the epidemic in these Southeast Asian countries are not nearly as grim as the situations reported for China and India. Official figures released by the government of China in 2003 suggest that there are some 840,000 cases of HIV/AIDS, but informed observers maintain that this figure grossly underestimates the extent of the epidemic and that a more realistic assessment would be on the order of 1.5 million cases and perhaps far more (Yardley 2006).[5] Most of the recent cases (and the lion's share overall) have occurred among individuals directly involved in intravenous drug use, heterosexual prostitution, or both, but a deeply alarming trend is the number of newly contracted cases among monogamous women who have been infected with the virus by husbands who inject drugs or have sex with prostitutes. As in Shanghai, the proliferation of increased socioeconomic disparities stemming from China's opening up to capitalist market forces has witnessed a surge in divorce and both pre- and extramarital relationships, along with sharp increases in rates of most sexually transmitted diseases.

India, whose population is nearly as large as China's (approximately 1.1 billion compared to roughly 1.3 billion), appears to have around 5.7 million people living with HIV/AIDS, hence more than four—and perhaps over eight—times as many cases per capita (depending on which of the previously cited Chinese figures one views as realistic). As in China, the bulk of the confirmed cases involve intravenous drug use, heterosexual prostitution, or both. As in China, too, a particularly disturbing trend is the number of new cases involving monogamous women who contract the virus from husbands who use drugs intravenously or frequent prostitutes. One of the problems here is that married men in India and elsewhere in South Asia often feel that monogamous expectations in marriage pertain only to their wives and since they are the primary "breadwinners" in their households they are free to spend "discretionary rupees" as they wish, even if this means engaging the services of prostitutes.

Another country likely to experience a devastating AIDS epidemic is Nepal, a landlocked Hindu kingdom located in the Himalayas, which shares extremely porous borders with India and China. The various ethnic groups comprising Nepal's population have been subject to dramatic socioeconomic and political changes in recent decades, many of which have undermined rural economic institutions and traditional caste occupations that in earlier times helped ensure livelihoods and security. One consequence of these changes is that about 40 percent of the county's population lives in poverty. In the absence of political and economic security and with little hope of a better tomorrow, the last few decades have seen hundreds of thousands of highland-dwelling Nepalis resettling in the country's plains or immigrating to India, where they seek employment in any sector of the Indian economy that can accommodate them. For many Nepalese women, such relocation has involved short- or long-term employment in brothels in Mumbai (Bombay) and other Indian cities, where, partly because of low rates of condom use, they are likely to contract HIV and other STDs. When women infected with STDs return to Nepal, settle down, and marry, they frequently transmit diseases to their husbands and children, which is one reason why the repatriation of Nepali women from Mumbai brothels in 1996 was attacked for "making Nepal a dumping site for AIDS" (Pradahn 1992 cited in Pike 2002:229). In any event, the number of persons currently infected with HIV/AIDS in Nepal exceeds 75,000. This is a daunting figure in light of the country's relatively small population of about 28 million, all the more so since the dynamics of global tourism and international mountaineering have created conditions conducive to its dramatic increase in the years to come (Ortner 1999).

The situation is especially acute among low-ranking and "untouchable" *dalit* caste groups such as the Badi, which have witnessed greatly reduced demand for the occupational services they traditionally provided other castes (musical entertainment and dancing at weddings, as well as fishing and net making). These dynamics have contributed to circumstances in which many Badi women have turned to commercial sex work to support themselves and their families, one result being the circulation of numerous discourses throughout Nepal that depict all Badi as polluted and contaminating members of a "prostitute caste." The resulting stigma and discrimination they experience in the educational and employment arenas and all varieties of public space clearly exacerbate the hardships they confront on a daily basis (Pike 2002).

In Nepal and elsewhere, the burdens of diseases such as AIDS are invariably borne more heavily by women (and girls) than by men (and boys), even in settings where males are more likely to contract the viruses that cause the diseases in question. This is partly because of gendered divisions of labor that assign women and girls most of the responsibility for feeding, nursing, and otherwise caring for sick and elderly members of the household. These responsibilities are often accorded more importance than regular attendance at school and in places of employment and thus undercut consistency in females' participation in formal schooling and workplace activities. The latter dynamics, in turn, contribute to scenarios wherein millions of women in South Asia and elsewhere come to marriage and experience the institution on an unequal economic footing in relation to their husbands. These dynamics greatly restrict women's horizons.

Rape, Abduction, and Body Politics in "Fundamentalism," Warfare, and Terror (India, Pakistan, Bangladesh, and Sri Lanka)

In modern Asia and many other parts of the world, military strategists, state-sponsored mobs, and relatively autonomous groups of vigilantes have increasingly turned to the abduction and rape of women and various forms of sexual torture to achieve their military, political, and psychological objectives. Scholarly and humanitarian research on these topics has yielded extremely distressing data on gendered and sexual violence directed against pregnant women and females of all ages and in some cases (e.g., the American-run Abu Ghraib prison in Iraq) males. Some of the most chilling accounts of this violence are contained in the narratives of women taken as hostages following decolonization in South Asia and the creation in 1947 of the two artificially bounded states of India and Pakistan. In the years immediately following the partition of India and Pakistan, more than thirty-three thousand Hindu and Sikh women were abducted by Muslim men and around fifty thousand Muslim women were abducted by either Hindu or Sikh men (Das 1995:215), mostly in the Punjab. These women were forced into sexual relations and marriage by their captors and in many cases bore them children. The horror and shame they experienced was greatly magnified by the reactions of family members and others back home, who tended to regard them as dishonored, defiled, and polluting, a source of unspeakable shame to their kinsmen, natal communities, and coreligionists. Testifying to a common scenario, one woman, when "rescued" and offered her "freedom," responded, "You have come to save us . . . [and] take us back to our relatives. You tell us that our relatives are eagerly waiting to receive us. You do not know our society. It is hell. They will kill us. Therefore, do not send us back" (224). Partly because of the strongly held local conviction that "the fruits of sexual violence should not be visible," many of the family narratives that the anthropologist Veena Das collected "dwelt at great length on the sacrifices of women who had chosen death by drowning themselves in wells, swallowing poison obtained by crushing their glass bangles, or in extreme cases begging their men to kill them with their own hands as an act of compassion" (218, 227). In sum, many of these women chose violent death for themselves rather than return to live among kin whose codes of honor and purity would have rendered their lives extremely difficult at best.

Developments in South Asia in more recent times are in many instances even more chilling, fueled as they have often been by the rise and spread in the late twentieth century of religious and ethnonationalist sentiments sometimes referred to under the rubric of "fundamentalism."[6] Bangladesh's War of Liberation in 1971 (the Muktijuddho), for example, resulted in the deaths of about half a million Bengali, Pakistani, and Indian soldiers and another half million civilians, the majority of whom, like the refugees the war created, were Bengali women and children. Included among the victims of this war were approximately two hundred thousand Bengali girls and women who were sexually abused and raped by soldiers (mostly Pakistani). In 1972, the Bangladeshi state formally designated the "200,000 mothers and sisters" as war heroines (birangonas), partly in an effort to pay homage to their sacrifices and partly to help mitigate the social ostracism they faced and thus facilitate their marriages and return to some semblance of a normal life (Mookherjee 2003). Unfortunately, the services provided by state-sponsored abortion clinics and centers for vocational training were quickly curtailed. Media coverage likewise declined dramatically, at least until the early 1990s when a furor erupted in connection with the trial of a man considered to have been a collaborator with the Pakistani army who, in the years following his apparent collaboration, had been reinstated in Bangladeshi political arenas. Since 1992, public discourse in Bangladesh has again focused on the *birangona*s, some of whom have written accounts of their experiences during the war and the subsequent trials and tribulations they have endured in the course of renegotiating the terms of their lives (e.g., Nilima Ibrahim's *Ami Birangona Bolchi* [*This Is the War Heroine Speaking*] 1994, 1995). The past decade has also seen important social science research by Bangladeshis and others aimed at collecting oral histories and thus giving voice to the victims of the war. Some of these scholarly efforts have resulted in the creation of web sites and related media products devoted both to the politics of remembrance and to considerations of the ethical issues involved in representing narratives of sexual violence (Mookherjee 2003).

Consider also events in the Indian state of Gujarat in February 2002, when a fire on a train said by some "official sources" to have been set by Muslims led to the deaths of fifty-eight Hindus. Within a few days of the fire, which a subsequent investigation revealed had started accidentally, retaliation by mobs of angered Hindus resulted in the deaths of between eight hundred and two thousand Muslims and widespread destruction of property that left over one hundred thousand people, mostly Muslims, homeless. During the conflagration, mobs, believed by many to have been "trained in rape," went on a rampage, generally unrestrained by the police who "told terrified groups of fleeing Muslims: 'We have no orders to save you'" (Baldwin 2002:187). "Groups of women were stripped naked and then made to run for miles, before being gang-raped and burnt alive. In some cases religious symbols were carved onto their bodies" (185). As one observer, Harsh Mander, later reported, "I have never known a riot which has used the sexual subjugation of women so widely as an instrument of violence. There are reports everywhere of [the] gang rape of young girls and women, often in the presence of members of their families, followed by their murder by being burned alive" (cited in Baldwin 2002:185).

One set of accounts that is permanently etched in the memories of many Gujaratis and other Indians concerns Kausar Bano, a Muslim woman, nine months pregnant, who was set upon by a Hindu crowd some three thousand strong. According to one eyewitness, "I was running [and] I saw a pregnant woman's belly being cut open . . . The fetus was pulled out and thrown up in the air. As it came down it was collected on the tip of the sword." The fetus was then thrown into the fire, as was Kausar. According to Ruth Baldwin, "The image of Kausar and her unborn child has assumed a dual meaning, for both Hindu aggressors and Muslim victims: The humiliation of the enemy through violation of the female body, and the assault on the future of the Muslim community through the destruction of the next generation" (2002:186).

Baldwin asks, "Why is gender violence such a consistent feature of the communal riots that spasmodically grip India?" Drawing on the insights of the Indian sociologist Raka Roy, her answer implicates the hierarchical caste system, with its emphasis on inequality and the inferiority of the Other, as well as entrenched beliefs

> that women are not only inferior, but also [that] women's sexuality has to be patrolled so that it is legitimately accessible to some men and inaccessible to others. If a woman's body belongs not to herself but to her community, then the violation of that body signifies an attack upon the honor (*izzat*) of the whole community. Hindu nationalists raped and burned minority women to destroy not only their bodies, but also the integrity and identity of Muslim society, the inferior Other. (2002:186–87)

In some ways most distressing, however, is the fact that "it was the complicity of the state," specifically, "Hindu nationalist organizations including the Baratya Janata Party (BJP), which heads the Gujarat state government," that made possible the mass rape and other violence. The state's inadequate provisioning of refugee camps, which, worldwide, are home mostly to women and children, has aggravated the situation. Making matters worse is that when the camps close the only option available to many of their residents is to "return to their villages, to live as second-class citizens in the ruins of their homes amongst the men who raped their sisters, burned their children, and killed their friends" (187). Unfortunately, the strategic use of rape in projects of genocide is globally widespread, as indicated by reports from Bosnia and Darfur and numerous other locales in Africa and elsewhere.

In recent decades, Sri Lanka has also witnessed broadly similar patterns of communal strife and gendered violence, although the chief protagonists in this case are the ethnic Sinhalese Theravada Buddhist majority, on the one hand, and the Tamil-speaking Hindu minority on the other. The Tamil secessionist movement and more encompassing civil war that have gripped this former colony for the past few decades have given rise to some of the most horrendous incidents of fratricidal violence and brutality on record for the twentieth century (Tambiah 1992). After independence in 1948, the Sinhalese nationalism that had developed in colonial times came to be redirected at ethnic Others, especially the Tamil minority. More generally, as

Jayawardena and de Alwis (1996) observe, the ethnonationalist mythologies of each of the major protagonists depict ethnic Others as destroying their Golden Age, "corrupting . . . [its] pristine purity, . . .[and] represent[ing] the threat of rape and thereby the possible 'pollution' of the 'daughters of the soil' . . . [in a context in which] the woman-mother symbolises the sacred, inviolable borders of the nation" (cited in Marecek 2000:146). The centrality of idealized women in myths such as these helps explain why attacks on one or another ethnic group or ethnicized national entity frequently focus on women and their bodies, specifically targeting corporeal symbols of women's dual capacity to glorify and reproduce the nation as well as defile and dishonor it. By the same token, the cultural logics of these myths help clarify why defenders of variously defined groups who feel themselves under siege from ethnic or racial Others go to great—sometimes brutal—lengths to police women and their bodies along with the always moral and inherently political boundaries between the public and private spheres in which they negotiate the terms of their lives.

One should not assume, however, that men alone are everywhere the perpetrators of these kinds of physical and symbolic violence or that women alone are the victims. "In all ethnic groups in Sri Lanka, some women have embraced nationalist causes and some have been active combatants. Perhaps the most publicized examples are the numerous female cadres of the L.T.T.E. [Liberation Tigers of Tamil Elam] who have functioned as assassins and suicide bombers. (Two of the most visible are the female suicide bombers who assassinated Rajiv Gandhi in India and President Ranasinghe Premadasa in Sri Lanka.)" (Maracek 2000:155). To help round out the picture, we might note that "Sinhala and Muslim women have functioned as interrogators in . . . prison camps . . . [and] have not stepped back from using torture;" and that "[i]n village massacres in border territories, women and children of all ethnic groups have participated in the carnage alongside men" (155–156).

While in many ways, then, women in Sri Lanka, as elsewhere, have been deeply implicated in ethnonationalist projects, the larger point is that "not all suffering can be attributed to generic 'men'; each ethnic group has suffered because of the acts of members (men and women) of other ethnic groups. Indeed, the suffering of some women (e.g., the conscription of their children) is instrumental to the suffering of other women. Thus, dichotomies such as women versus men, victims versus agents, domination versus freedom, and perhaps even peace versus war are too simplistic" (156).

Social Activism in an Age of Global Connection (Indonesia)

Discussions of militarization, prostitution, and the ravages of the AIDS pandemic make for grim reading. So, too, do accounts of the widespread use of rape, sexual torture, and abduction as instruments of strategy in warfare and terror. Fortunately there is also some cause for optimism, for throughout Asia bodies are also widely deployed in the pursuit of variously defined goals of social justice, equality, and environmentally friendly ("green") economic development. In short, tens, if not hundreds, of millions of Asians (men, women, and the transgendered alike) are routinely putting their bodies on the line in pursuit of a better tomorrow.

These dynamics are evident throughout South Asia, a point well worth bearing in mind in light of the discussion in the preceding pages.[7] But they are perhaps nowhere more apparent than in Indonesia, a country encompassing some thirteen thousand islands that is home to more Muslims than any other and boasts the fourth-largest population in the world (over 235 million people). The political and religious violence that has wracked many parts of Indonesia in recent years (and has included the strategic use of rape to achieve military, political, and psychological objectives [see, e.g., Strassler 2004]) has received most of the international media coverage afforded the archipelago. But the country has also seen a phenomenal fluorescence of social activism and civic pluralism since the 1980s and the fall of despotic President Suharto (r. 1966–98) in particular. Indeed, there is a largely untold story of vibrant dialogue among a cast of arguably strange (or at least surprising) bedfellows who for the most part toil quietly, and without attention from afar, to maintain control of their variously construed communities and local resources. They include rock-climbers and nature lovers of different stripes; conservation biologists and natural scientists in other fields, as well as "tree huggers" and other environmental activists; local community leaders and lobbyists for indigenous rights; Muslim intellectuals and feminists (both secular and Muslim); paralegals, lawyers, and human rights workers, including advocates for gays, lesbians, bisexuals, and the transgendered; and spokespeople for the preservation of the archipelago's historic architecture and rich cultural legacies. Anna Tsing (2005:22, 26, 224 passim) has recently written of the tremendous synergy created by these groups and the promise of "intercultural hybridity" that helps animate the diverse forms of advocacy that Indonesians who have "form[ed] bridges across regional languages and across sectors of society" have struggled to create in recent decades, especially in the context of development organizations, issue-oriented activism, and democratic agitation. Tsing's account of "coalitions built on awkwardly linked compatibilities" fully acknowledges the forces of imperial power but also presents compelling portraits of present-day utopian dynamics and the possibilities they hold for the future (267; see also Hefner 2000: and Bowen 2003).

Indonesia's burgeoning civil society includes a number of progressive Muslim organizations, some of which have developed or embraced explicitly feminist agendas. One of the best-known organizations, founded in Jakarta in 1983 by a prominent lawyer and religious scholar, Masdar Mas'udi, is the Society for Pesantren and Community Development (Perhimpunan Pengembangan Pesantren dan Masyarakat), commonly known as P3M. The chief concern of P3M has always been to organize community development and rural education programs and run them through the vast network of Islamic boarding schools (*pesantren*) overseen by the "traditionalist" Muslim association Nahdlatul Ulama. While P3M was not originally conceived with a focus on gender or women's rights, by 1994 its leadership had enlisted the assistance of a well-known feminist activist, Lies Marcoes-Natsir, to initiate community-oriented programs geared toward improving the living standards, reproductive rights, and overall health and well-being of Muslim women in accordance with contemporary reinterpretations of sacred religious texts (Marcoes-Natsir 2000; Brenner 2005). Its outreach activities and widely accessible writings on Islam and issues of equality, justice, and democracy bode well for Muslim and other women in Indonesia, particularly since they are drawing women into public and specifically political arenas in new and productive ways.

Like university-educated Muslim feminists in many other parts of the world, the women centrally involved in the feminist programs of P3M have endeavored to promote alternative readings of foundational Islamic texts such as the Quran and the *hadith*. These scholarly efforts are aimed at recuperating the egalitarian ethical and legal sensibilities of early Islam that were stifled by more hierarchical readings of classic texts, the latter of which gained ascendancy in the course of the formal codification and official elaboration of Islamic law and "custom" that occurred in the centuries after the deaths of the Prophet and his companions. Drawing also on the liberal sensibilities of global feminism and transnational nongovernmental organizations (NGOs) concerned with the quality of women's lives, the members of P3M's women's wing have campaigned vigorously to ensure greater legal and basic human rights for Muslim women, devoting much of their energy to ameliorating problems associated with polygyny, abandonment, and the mistreatment of women in the context of marriage and divorce, as well as STDs, rape, illegal abortions, and the like. They have done so mostly by organizing high-profile workshops and conferences, by writing letters to the editors of major dailies, by publishing pamphlets and books, and by formal and informal lobbying efforts of various kinds.

The bottom line is that because of their adept engagement in coalition politics—their members work closely with Islamic scholars and religious leaders, as well as officials in various ministries and the executive branch, on legislative and policy matters concerning women and religion—their influence is enormous. (That said, some ordinary Muslims and others regard them as too radical, too feminist, or too Western in their approaches to textual interpretation, advocacy, and reform.) More generally, P3M promotes a vision of Islam that is highly principled, inclusive, and pluralistic, as do many of its counterparts in Malaysia, Pakistan, Bangladesh, India, and other Asian countries. These organizations have contributed a great deal to the cultivation and "scaling up" of sentiments and dispositions that are conducive to the expansion of civil society, and in all likelihood they will continue to do so in the years ahead.[8]

5

Conclusion

The patterns and processes described in this booklet illustrate the range of the diversity in gender, sexuality, and body politics that exists in modern Asian societies and cultures, just as they shed light on commonalities throughout the region. In these concluding remarks, I summarize and elaborate briefly on some of the commonalities at issue and raise a series of questions about possible scenarios for the future. These similarities include the ubiquity of religious ideologies that accord greater prestige to males and thus legitimize male privilege and diverse modalities of gender inequality; the widespread distribution, except in Southeast Asia, of structures of kinship and marriage entailing patriliny, patrilocality, and various kinds of patrifocal emphases; the increasing prevalence of modern factories in search of exploitable daughters and other females whose wages, though generally lower than those afforded their male kin and certainly paltry by most standards, are nonetheless a great boon to their natal families and households; the emergence and growing popularity of hybrid wedding ceremonies that prominently feature Western (specifically Christian) symbols and idioms, indexing both the bridal couple's cosmopolitanism and to a lesser extent their ostensible commitment to companionate marriage involving a modicum of equality between husband and wife, as well as the relative autonomy of the married couple vis-à-vis larger circles of "blood" and affinal kin; growing concerns with both the quantity and "racial" quality of children born and raised, especially in places such as potentially labor-short Singapore, which can ill afford declining birthrates and fears a weakening of its national (Chinese/Confucian) fiber; and the widespread favoring of sons and attendant discrimination against daughters, particularly in East and South Asia, certain regions of which have recently witnessed rises (most notably in the relatively wealthy and educated sectors of society) in both female-selective abortion and the skewed sex ratios of infants and young children as a whole. As with others noted below, many of these dynamics attest to patterns of stratified reproduction involving cultural political relations that favor certain groups' nurturance and biological and social reproduction while discouraging or precluding those of others.

We have also seen that in various Asian contexts prior to the twentieth century individuals held to have special spiritual and ritual powers were frequently involved in transgender practices and/or same-sex relations; that the latter practices and relations were accorded legitimacy in some contexts, just as certain classes of people who embodied or championed them were seen as having direct links to the sacred; that in many present-day settings the practices and relations at issue tend to be regarded by society as a whole as "no big deal" in the sense that, at least by Western standards, they are not seriously stigmatized or criminalized (so long as the individuals involved uphold other basic community norms); and that, even in the more patriarchal and gender-inegalitarian societies of East Asia, nineteenth-century sexualities were more fluid than they are at present. More generally, the dichotomous categorization of all individuals as either "heterosexuals" (normal/normative) or "homosexuals" (deviant/nonnormative)—or as normatively gendered "males" or "females"—is largely a product of late-nineteenth and early twentieth-century medical and scientific discourses on sex elaborated in the Western academic disciplines that came to be subsumed under the rubric of sexology. These binaries took root in the West and spread throughout Asia and the rest of the world in the late nineteenth and early twentieth centuries in the context of Western imperial expansions that helped showcase Western science, technology, and military prowess throughout Asia and the rest of what came to be known as the Third World and subsequently the global South.

In recent decades, forces of transnational capitalism and globalization, including the notoriously ungovernable Internet, have contributed to the circulation throughout Asia of Western-origin discourses bearing on genders, bodies, and sexualities. And in some places (I mentioned China, Taiwan, Singapore, and Indonesia, but the list is actually much longer) feminist-inflected narratives bearing on women, gender, and sexual rights as human rights have helped animate largely homegrown movements aimed at contesting gender and sexual arrangements entailed in conventional kinship and marriage. Also contributing to dramatic change but often working at cross-purposes to the movements noted here are agents of corporate capitalisms who seek to capture gay markets ("pink dollars") and exploit other commercial opportunities either by creating forms of entertainment dramatizing sexual or gender ambiguity or by focusing media attention on whatever sells, be it vociferous advocacy of feminism or sexual rights, their denigration, or both. We have also seen that large-scale sex industries accompany the massing of military forces and are thus primed to become sites of global (sex) tourism, and that social dislocations caused by widespread poverty, uneven economic development, and military conflict and terror in particular create conditions conducive to rape, torture, and abduction, as well as epidemics of sexually transmitted disease such as AIDS.

86

Asians are also putting their bodies on the line in social activism on behalf of progressive causes, doing so in ways that promise great hope for the future. An important question that arises here concerns the future of struggles for gender and sexual equality in Asia and their relationship to similarly oriented movements in the West. In the United States, to take one Western example, the civil rights movement helped set the stage for variously defined women's movements, all such collective struggles helping to pave the way for the battles currently being waged over gay marriage and other forms of sexual equality. Progressions of this sort, like those involving the succession of juridical discourses bearing on sexuality that Foucault (1978) documents for eighteenth- and nineteenth-century France and other parts of Europe, are by no means inevitable in Asia, even though there are some fascinating parallels. To paraphrase Manderson and Jolly (1997:22), we need to be wary of discursive genealogies and "theories of development which conceive a teleological trajectory" whereby the West becomes "a dress rehearsal for the rest of the world." There are numerous reasons why historical trajectories in Asia may not be analogous to those in the West. One reason is that in Asia, as in many other regions of the world, cultural political responses to the onslaught of globalization and neoimperialism emanating from the West entail powerful (re)assertions of moralities that are simultaneously represented and experienced as "indigenous," "traditional," and vehemently "anti-Western." Discourses of "Asian values" articulated in the 1990s by Mahathir Mohamad, Lee Kuan Yew, Shintaro Ishihara, and other Asian leaders and their charges provide examples of this. Another relevant dynamic is the heightened normativity in all domains of social life that is seen by Asia's political elites as necessary to sustain the new Asian capitalisms, to negotiate the rise of various forms of religious or ethnonationalistic "fundamentalism," and to contend with the aftermath of September 11 and the vicissitudes of the U.S. "war on terror." The history of the region makes it clear that these developments will inform myriad dynamics bearing on genders, sexualities, and body politics, though precisely how they will do so remains to be seen.

Notes

Chapter 2

[1] Bogang (a pseudonym) was the main site of my field research during the periods 1978–80 and 1987–88.

[2] Some of these contrasts are keyed to variations in systems of production, exchange, prestige, and personhood. For additional information on these and related matters, see Peletz 1995, 1996, 2002.

[3] The household survey I conducted in Bogang in 1979 and 1980 revealed that roughly two-thirds of all completed marriages had ended in divorce. Similar patterns have been reported by scholars working in other regions of the peninsula, but recent decades have seen a decline in divorce in most areas of the country.

[4] Malays rarely gamble or consume alcohol, two activities that are proscribed by Islam, but it is men rather than women who constitute the exceptions to the rule.

[5] Limitations of space preclude consideration of other Malay gender categories such as those utilized to refer to feminized males and masculinized females (*pondan*), male-bodied transsexuals (*mak nyah*), and women who have sex with women (*tomboys*, *peng kids*, etc.). Some of these terms are discussed briefly later on.

[6] Practical discourses on gender that are analogous to those of Malay Muslims also exist among Burmese Buddhists, but their contours and specifics are not clear from Spiro's work. For these reasons and because of space limitations, I do not attempt to delineate their basic features. For similar reasons, I do not engage their counterparts among the Hindu communities considered below.

[7] For a review of the more encompassing dynamics, see Ong 1991.

[8] I use the term "Korea" here as shorthand for the Republic of Korea (South Korea). Unfortunately, little is known about gender relations and sexuality in the Democratic People's Republic of Korea (North Korea). For an overview of the available research on North Korean women, see Ryang 2000.

[9] I am grateful to Hyun Ok Park for bringing these sources to my attention.

[10] Unless otherwise noted, the material quoted in this section derives from Agence France-Presse 2003.

[11] In some parts of Asia, observance of Valentine's Day is highly contested. In India, for instance, valentines are routinely burned at right-wing political rallies scheduled around the holiday. Groups opposed to observance of Valentine's Day on the grounds that it represents the growing influence of Western values in India have repeatedly attacked restaurants, hotels, gift shops, and other establishments that celebrate or promote the holiday. (See, for example, Rabinowitz 2007.)

[12] I say "usually" because allowances are made for Buddhist monks and the members of certain other religious orders who neither marry nor engage in sexual relations but are nonetheless considered to be adults.

[13] Rates of abortion in Vietnam are among the highest in the world, with some studies indicating as many as 1,700 abortions per 1,000 live births (Bich 1999:193). Most Vietnamese women who seek abortions are married, have two or more children, and are between thirty and forty years old. Data bearing primarily on women in this age group indicate that in 1992 the "total abortion rate for the country was at least 2.5 per woman" and that "if the trend continues, there will be twice as many abortions as births annually in the near future" (193–194; see also Croll 2000:48). Preferences for sons contribute to the prevalence of abortion, but many other factors are involved. These include state policies forbidding sex education in schools, which result in a lack of reliable information among curious, sexually active youth; the difficulty, especially in rural areas, of purchasing condoms; and the widespread reliance on intrauterine devices (IUDs)—which are generally less efficacious than condoms—to prevent conception. In short, partly because IUDs are commonplace but not as extensively used as they might be, so too are abortions. It remains to add that IUDs are ineffective in preventing the spread of sexually transmitted diseases (STDs) such as HIV/AIDS; that partly for this reason Vietnam is now confronting an alarming epidemic of HIV/AIDS; and that the epidemic is spreading to the general population, though it is currently concentrated among sex workers, their clients, and their clients' regular partners, on the one hand, and among intravenous drug users and their partners on the other.

Chapter 3

[1] Some of the relevant issues are taken up in Peletz 2006 and the sources cited there.

[2] Ann Gold has noted that "at a higher level to understand her [the female goddess] as simultaneously wielding weapons and full of grace is an important theological and devotional truth." A more general point is that in Hinduism "the grace-giving element of female deities is fused with the fearsome" to a greater degree than suggested by many conventional depictions of female capacities to devour and destroy (personal communication, August 13, 2006, and October 31, 2006; see also Gold 2007).

[3] The Bohemian Grove, owned and operated by the Bohemian Club of San Francisco, is a private, wooded compound of several thousand acres located on the Russian River in Sonoma County that for over a century has served as a "retreat" for men from California and elsewhere who belong to the upper echelons of the nation's political elite. Domhoff (1974) has produced the definitive study of the Bohemian Grove, whose members have included thousands of nationally prominent corporate leaders and captains of industry and many American presidents (including Hoover, Eisenhower, Nixon, Ford, Reagan, and George H. W. Bush). Research conducted by James Vaughn in the mid- to late 1990s makes it clear that cross-dressing by men (including the use of false breasts, wigs, heavy makeup, and skirts and dresses) still occurs in plays, skits, and other contexts (many of which involve bacchanalian rituals); that certain men make themselves up to look like drag queens while others seek to appear indistinguishable from "sexy" women; and that some of the men who participate in these retreats also engage in heterosexual prostitution in nearby towns (Vaughn 2006). As Domhoff (1974:27) observes and Vaughn's research indicates, many of the Bohemian Grove's myths, rituals, and symbols focus on sex; indeed, "the [latter] topic is outranked as a subject for light conversation only by remarks about drinking enormous quantities of alcohol and urinating on redwoods." Much of the humor at these kinds of retreats is misogynist and homophobic, a critically important reminder that not all gender-transgressive (or sexually transgressive) behavior is indicative of pluralistic sentiments or dispositions. The ways in which "othering" practices such as those that occur in the Bohemian Grove and other exclusively or predominantly male institutions (fraternities, the armed forces) contribute to male bonding and social cohesiveness of other kinds have been variously addressed by Domhoff and Vaughn as well as Gregor (1985) and Sanday (1990).

[4] Thais sometimes use the term *kathoey* to refer to female-bodied individuals, but this usage is not common.

[5] The term "gay" is widely used throughout Asia, but its meanings vary according to locale and sociolinguistic context and its connotations are not necessarily the same as those associated with its usage in English-language settings, though there is considerable overlap. In some circumstances, the term refers primarily to certain categories of phenotypic males (e.g., male-bodied transsexuals and their effeminate male counterparts) who have sex with other males; in many, perhaps most, others, it has broader meanings, denoting any male (or female-bodied) individual erotically oriented toward same-sex relations, who may or may not engage in heterosexual relations, including conventional marriage. Here and elsewhere in this booklet, I italicize terms such as "gay" (and "lesbian") when I seek to emphasize one or another Asian identity or Asian-language usage. I use roman type when deploying the terms to convey their now conventional English-language meanings (e.g., a person inclined toward erotic relations with others of the same sex). When quoting published material, I retain the author's conventions as I normally do when discussing that material. The sources cited in this chapter address many of the relevant issues bearing on these and other terminological, conceptual, and analytic matters.

[6] By some estimates, prior to the end of World War I Europe and America "held almost 85% of the entire world in the form of colonies, dependencies, mandates and subjugated territories" (Said 1988:ix).

Chapter 4

[1] This figure does not include fatalities of the 1915–18 Armenian genocide or the World War II era Holocaust; estimates of the latter deaths are noted below. The primary sources for the figures cited in this section, some of which are of arguable reliability, include the Peace Pledge Union based in the United Kingdom (http://www.ppu.org.uk/war/facts/www00-95a.html; accessed on April 24, 2006), and the atlas of twentieth-century death tolls compiled by Matthew White (last updated November 2005, http://users.erols.com/mwhite28/warstat1.htm, accessed on May 4, 2006). The Peace Pledge Union has reorganized its website since I downloaded material in April 2006 and is currently located at http://www.ppu.org.uk. I thank Ian Roxborough for discussing these issues with me and for bringing the relevant resources to my attention.

[2] Sources for these figures include Bishop and Robinson 1998:8, 19 passim; Boonchalaksi and Guest 1998:162; and Somswasdi 2004:1.

[3] The figures for HIV/AIDS that are cited in this booklet derive from the World Health Organization's (WHO) Global Health Atlas (2007), unless

otherwise noted. The most current set of figures that are available from WHO were collected in 2005 and updated in December 2006. These figures are available online from the WHO website located at http://www.who.int/globalatlas/default.asp.

[4] Although the Subic Bay Naval Base and other U.S. military installations in the Philippines were formally closed in the early 1990s, the United States maintains a large military presence in the country, with most American troops posted at Philippine bases (Lutz 2006). In short, the dynamics Enloe describes prevail well beyond the Subic Bay area and continue to exist in many areas of the country.

[5] In January 2006, official Chinese sources suggested that the figure of 840,000 was an overestimate and that the more accurate figure was around 650,000 cases (Yardley 2006). Knowledgeable experts are even more skeptical about the veracity of this claim.

[6] I have placed the term "fundamentalism" in scare quotes to signal its problematic nature when used to refer to religious and political phenomena outside the Protestant American context that gave rise to the concept in the early twentieth century. Generally speaking, Protestant fundamentalists (sometimes referred to as Christian fundamentalists) are those who believe that sacred scriptures such as the Bible require literal interpretation because they contain the verbatim words of God. This basic orienting belief is what distinguishes them from other Protestants as well as members of other Christian denominations (e.g., Catholics) who are not fundamentalists. One problem with using this term to designate followers of other religious faiths, such as Islam, is that all Muslims take the Quran to be the literal word of God (as revealed to the Prophet Muhammad by the archangel Gabriel). Hence, terms such as "fundamentalism" and "fundamentalist" are meaningless, misleading, or worse when applied to Muslims or Islam. The problems are compounded by the widespread tendency in the West to elide distinctions among fundamentalists, activists, militants, and terrorists, especially in discussions of Islam.

[7] The more general theme to bear in mind here has to do with a caveat noted in the introduction. While some sections of this booklet involve exploration of topics that are iconically associated with certain locales (e.g., communal violence in South Asia and the sex industry in Thailand), I am not suggesting that communal violence occurs only in South Asia or that the skin trade exists solely in Thailand. The majority of the subjects addressed in this booklet could be examined in the context of a single Asian country. Because this is not possible here and some subjects have been more thoroughly investigated

in certain regions than others, I capitalize on the strengths of the extant scholarship and offer readers a portrait of gender and sexuality in modern Asia in the form of a mosaic crafted to fit topical pieces and locales together, albeit without any assumption that these mappings are primordial, transhistorical, or exclusive. Mosaics of alternative cast and design are certainly feasible.

[8] It is arguably ironic that a few years after the founder and director of P3M published an important book on Islam and women's reproductive rights (*Islam dan Hak-Hak Reproduksi Peremupan: Dialog Fiqih Pemberdayaan* [*Islam and Women's Reproductive Rights: A Dialogue of the Islamic Jurisprudence of Empowerment*] [1997]) he took a second wife. "That someone known as an outspoken advocate for women's rights had quietly indulged in . . . [the] practice [of polygyny] sent shock waves through the Islamic feminist community and especially through P3M. A number of its staff members resigned in protest, some joining or participating in the creation of other organizations . . . to carry on the activities in the area of women's rights for which P3M had been known. This event served as a painful reminder of the considerable obstacles, both practical and ideological, faced by the proponents of Islamic feminism in Indonesia" (Brenner 2005:115). For a discussion of other obstacles (philosophical, moral, and political) confounding the relationship between feminism and Islam, see Saba Mahmood's *Politics of Piety: The Islamic Revival and the Feminist Subject* (2005), which focuses on women's extensive involvement in Islamist movements in Egypt but is clearly relevant to an understanding of women and Islam in Indonesia and other Asian settings. Mahmood (31 passim) argues that discourses of secular-liberal feminism that originate in the West or are unwittingly grounded in Western secular-liberal assumptions concerning the ostensibly autonomous, highly individuated subject are largely incapable of coming to terms with women's participation in socially conservative Islamist movements in which "submission to certain forms of (external) authority is a condition for achieving the subject's potentiality." Some readers may feel that Mahmood overgeneralizes from a very particular, late-twentieth-century variant of hyperindividualist secular liberalism to (neo)liberal thought in general, but she correctly identifies an important range of dynamics that make for an uneasy relationship between certain streams of Western-style feminism and various impulses in contemporary Islamic ethics and politics.

Works Cited

Note: The sources cited here represent a very small portion of the relevant English-language literature. Additional sources are listed in "Suggestions for Further Reading" but limitations of space require that I exclude many major works in the field.

Abu-Lughod, Lila. 1986. *Veiled Sentiments: Honor and Poetry in a Bedouin Society*. Berkeley: University of California Press.

Agence France-Presse. 2003. "Singapore Classifies Romance as a National Security Issue." *New York Times*, February 13.

Agrawal, Anuja. 1997. "Gendered Bodies: The Case of the 'Third Gender' in India." *Contributions to Indian Sociology*, n.s., 31(2): 273–97.

Altman, Dennis. 1996. "Rupture or Continuity? The Internationalization of Gay Identities." *Social Text* 48: 77–94.

———. 2001. *Global Sex*. Chicago: University of Chicago Press.

Andaya, Barbara. 1994. "The Changing Religious Role of Women in Premodern Southeast Asia." *South East Asia Research* 2(2): 99–116.

Andaya, Barbara, ed. 2000. *Other Pasts: Women, Gender, and History in Early Modern Southeast Asia*. Honolulu: Center for Southeast Asian Studies, University of Hawai'i.

Andaya, Leonard. 2000. "The Bissu: Study of a Third Gender in Indonesia." In *Other Pasts*, ed. Barbara Andaya, 27–46. Honolulu: Center for Southeast Asian Studies, University of Hawai'i.

Appadurai, Arjun. 1986. "Theory in Anthropology: Center and Periphery." *Comparative Studies in Society and History* 28(2): 356–61.

Atkinson, Jane, and Shelly Errington, eds. 1990. *Power and Difference: Gender in Island Southeast Asia*. Stanford: Stanford University Press.

Baldwin, Ruth. 2002. "Gujarat's Gendered Violence." In *Nothing Sacred: Women Respond to Religious Fundamentalism and Terror*, ed. Betsy Reed, 185–87. New York: Thunder's Mouth/Nation Books.

Beatty, Andrew. 2002. "Changing Places: Relatives and Relativism in Java." *Journal of the Royal Anthropological Institute*, n.s., 8: 469–91.

Belak, Brenda. 2002. *Gathering Strength: Women from Burma on Their Rights*. Chiangmai: Images Asia.

Bich, Pham Van. 1999. *The Vietnamese Family in Change: The Case of the Red River Delta*. Richmond, Surrey: Curzon.

Bishop, Ryan, and Lillian Robinson. 1998. *Night Market: Sexual Cultures and the Thai Economic Miracle*. New York: Routledge.

Blackwood, Evelyn. 1999. "Tombois in West Sumatra." In *Female Desires: Same-Sex Relations and Transgender Practices across Cultures*, ed. Evelyn Blackwood and Saskia Wieringa, 181–205. New York: Columbia University Press.

———. 2005. "Gender Transgression in Colonial and Post-colonial Indonesia." *Journal of Asian Studies* 64: 849-80.

Boellstorff, Tom. 1999. "The Perfect Path: Gay Men, Marriage, Indonesia." *QLQ: A Journal of Lesbian and Gay Studies* 5(4): 475–510.

Boonchalaksi, Wathinee and Philip Guest. 1998. "Prostitution in Thailand." In *The Sex Sector: The Economic and Social Bases of Prostitution in Southeast Asia*, ed. Lin L. Lim, 130–69. Geneva: International Labor Organization.

Bornstein, Kate. 1995. *Gender Outlaw: On Men, Women, and the Rest of Us*. New York: Vintage.

Bourdieu, Pierre. 1977. *Outline of a Theory of Practice*. Cambridge: Cambridge University Press.

Bowen, John. 2003. *Islam, Law, and Equality in Indonesia: An Anthropology of Public Reasoning*. Cambridge: Cambridge University Press.

Brenner, Suzanne. 2005. "Islam and Gender Politics in Late New Order Indonesia." In *Spirited Politics: Religion and Public Life in Contemporary Southeast Asia*, ed. Andrew Willford and Kenneth George, 93–118. Ithaca: Southeast Asia Program, Cornell University.

Brooke, James. 2005. "Here Comes the Japanese Bride, Looking Very Western." *New York Times*, July 8.

Butler, Judith. 1993. *Bodies That Matter: On the Discursive Limits of "Sex."* New York: Routledge.

Cohen, Lawrence. 1995. "The Pleasures of Castration: The Postoperative Status of Hijras, Jankhas, and Academics." In *Sexual Nature/Sexual Culture: Theorizing Sexuality from the Perspective of Pleasure*, ed. Paul Abramson and Steven Pinkerton, 276–304. Chicago: University of Chicago Press.

Cohen, Shelee. 1995. "'Like a Mother to Them': Stratified Reproduction and West Indian Childcare Workers and Employers in New York." In *Conceiving the New World Order: The Global Politics of Reproduction*, ed. Faye Ginsburg and Rayna Rapp, 78–102. Berkeley: University of California Press.

Croll, Elisabeth. 2000. *Endangered Daughters: Discrimination and Development in Asia*. New York: Routledge.

Das, Veena. 1995. "National Honor and Practical Kinship: Unwanted Women and Children." In *Conceiving the New World Order: The Global Politics of Reproduction*, ed. Faye Ginsburg and Rayna Rapp, 212–33. Berkeley: University of California Press.

Denton, Lynn T. 2004. *Female Ascetics in Hinduism*. Albany: State University of New York Press.

Deveaux, Monique. 2000. *Cultural Pluralism and Dilemmas of Justice*. Ithaca: Cornell University Press.

Domhoff, G. William. 1974. *The Bohemian Grove and Other Retreats: A Study in Ruling-Class Cohesiveness*. New York: Harper and Row.

Duk-kun, Byun. 2003. "4 in 10 High-Schoolers Want Plastic Surgery." *Korea Times*, August 26.

Dwyer, Daisy. 1978. *Images and Self-Images: Male and Female in Morocco*. New York; Columbia University Press.

Enloe, Cynthia. 1990. *Bananas, Beaches, and Bases: Making Feminist Sense of International Politics*. Berkeley: University of California Press.

Errington, Shelly. 1989. *Meaning and Power in a Southeast Asian Realm*. Princeton: Princeton University Press.

Farquhar, Judith. 2002. *Appetites: Food and Sex in Post-socialist China*. Durham: Duke University Press.

Farrer, James. 2002. *Opening Up: Youth Sex Culture and Market Reform in Shanghai*. Chicago: University of Chicago Press.

Foucault, Michel. 1977. *Discipline and Punish: The Birth of the Prison*. New York: Vintage.

———. 1978. *The History of Sexuality,* Vol. I: *An Introduction*. New York: Vintage.

———. [1984] 1997. "Preface to *The History of Sexuality*, Volume Two." In *Essential Works of Foucault, 1954–1984*, Vol. I, *Ethics: Subjectivity and Truth*, ed. Paul Rabinow, 199–205. New York: New Press.

Geertz, Clifford. 2006. "Comment." *Current Anthropology* 47(2): 327–28.

Gold, Ann Grodzins. 2002. "Counterpoint Authority in Women's Ritual Expressions: A View from the Village." *In Jewels of Authority: Women and Textual Tradition in Hindu India*, ed. Laurie L. Patton, 177–201. New York: Oxford University Press.

———. 2007. "Gender." In *Studying Hinduism: Key Concepts and Methods*. ed. Sushil Mittal and Gene Thursby, 178-93. London: Routledge.

Greenberg, David F. 1988. *The Construction of Homosexuality*. Chicago: University of Chicago Press.

Gregor, Thomas. 1985. *Anxious Pleasures: The Sexual Lives of an Amazonian People*. Chicago: University of Chicago Press.

Hamabata, Matthews Masayuki. 1990. *Crested Kimono: Power and Love in the Japanese Business Family*. Ithaca: Cornell University Press.

Hefner, Robert. 2000. *Civil Islam: Muslims and Democratization in Indonesia*. Princeton: Princeton University Press.

Heng, Geraldine, and Janadas Devan. 1995. "State Fatherhood: The Politics of Sexuality, Race, and Nationalism in Singapore." In *Bewitching Women, Pious Men: Gender and Body Politics in Southeast Asia*, ed. Aihwa Ong and Michael G. Peletz, 195–215. Berkeley: University of California Press.

Ibrahim, Nilima. 1994, 1995. *Ami Birangona Bolchi [This is the War Heroine Speaking])*, Vols. 1 and 2. Dhaka: Jagriti.

Jackson, Peter A. 1997. "Kathoey < > Gay > < Man: The Historical Emergence of Gay Male Identity in Thailand." In *Sites of Desire, Economies of Pleasure: Sexualities in Asia and the Pacific*, ed. Lenore Manderson and Margaret Jolly, 166–90. Chicago: University of Chicago Press.

Jayawardena, Kumari, and Malathi de Alwis. 1996. *Embodied Violence: Communalising Women's Sexuality in South Asia*. London: Zed.

Jha, Prabhat, Rajesh Kumar, Priya Vasa, Neeraj Dhingra, Deva Thiruchelvam, and Rahim Moineddin. 2006. "Low Male-to-Female Sex Ration of Children Born in India: National Survey of 1.1 Million Households." *Lancet* 367: 211–18.

Johnson, Mark. 1997. *Beauty and Power: Transgendering and Cultural Transformation in the Southern Philippines*. Oxford: Berg.

Jost, John, and Brenda Major, eds. 2001. *The Psychology of Legitimacy: Emerging Perspectives on Ideology, Justice, and Intergroup Relations*. Cambridge: Cambridge University Press.

Kendall, Laurel. 1996. *Getting Married in Korea: Of Gender, Morality, and Modernity*. Berkeley: University of California Press.

Keun-min, Bae. 2005. "Appearance Not Everything but Still Something." *Korea Times*, March 25.

Keyes, Charles. 1984. "Mother or Mistress but Never a Monk: Buddhist Notions of Female Gender in Rural Thailand." *American Ethnologist* 11(2): 223–41.

Khandelwal, Meena. 2004. *Women in Ochre Robes: Gendering Hindu Renunciation*. Albany: State University of New York Press.

Khandelwal, Meena, Sondra Hausner, and Ann Grodzins Gold, eds. 2006. *Women's Renunciation in South Asia: Nuns, Yoginis, Saints, and Singers*. London: Palgrave.

Kibria, Nazli. 1993. *Family Tightrope: The Changing Lives of Vietnamese Americans*. Princeton: Princeton University Press.

Kirsch, Thomas. 1982. "Buddhism, Sex Roles, and the Thai Economy." In *Women of Southeast Asia*, ed. Penny Van Esterik, 16–41. DeKalb: Center for Southeast Asian Studies, Northern Illinois University.

———. 1985. "Text and Context: Buddhist Sex Roles/Culture of Gender Revisited." *American Ethnologist* 12(2): 302–20.

Kondo, Dorinne K. 1990. *Crafting Selves: Power, Gender, and Discourses of Identity in a Japanese Workplace*. Chicago University of Chicago Press.

Law, Lisa. 1997. "A Matter of 'Choice': Discourses on Prostitution in the Philippines." In *Sites of Desire, Economies of Pleasure: Sexualities in Asia and the Pacific*, ed. Lenore Manderson and Margaret Jolly, 233 –61. Chicago: University of Chicago Press.

Ledgerwood, Judy. 1994. "Gender Symbolism and Culture Change: Viewing the Virtuous Woman in the Khmer Story 'Mea Yoeng.'" In *Cambodian Culture since 1975: Homeland and Exile*, ed. May Ebihara, Carol Mortland, and Judy Ledgerwood, 119–28. Ithaca: Cornell University Press.

Lee Kuan Yew. 1983. "Talent for the Future." *Straits Times*, August 15.

Louie, Kam. 2002. *Theorising Chinese Masculinity: Society and Gender in China*. Cambridge: Cambridge University Press.

Lu, Sheldon H. 2000. "Soap Opera in China: The Transnational Politics of Visuality, Sexuality, and Masculinity." *Cinema Journal* 30(1): 25–47.

Lutz, Catherine. 2006. "Empire Is in the Details." *American Ethnologist* 33(4): 593–611.

Mackie, Vera. 2003. *Feminism in Modern Japan: Citizenship, Embodiment, and Sexuality*. Cambridge: Cambridge University Press.

Mahmood, Saba. 2005. *Politics of Piety: The Islamic Revival and the Feminist Subject*. Princeton: Princeton University Press.

Manalansan, Martin. 2003. *Global Divas: Filipino Gay Men in the Diaspora*. Durham: Duke University Press.

Manderson, Lenore. 1995. "The Pursuit of Pleasure and the Sale of Sex." In *Sexual Nature/Sexual Culture: Theorizing Sexuality from the Perspective of Pleasure*, ed. Paul Abramson and Steven Pinkerton, 305–29. Chicago: University of Chicago Press.

Manderson, Lenore, and Margaret Jolly. 1997. "Introduction: Sites of Desire/ Economies of Pleasure in Asia and the Pacific." In *Sites of Desire/Economies of Pleasure: Sexualities in Asia and the Pacific*, ed. Lenore Manderson and Margaret Jolly, 1–26. Chicago: University of Chicago Press.

Marcoes-Natsir, Lies. 2000. "Reproductive Health and Women's Rights from an Islamic Perspective: The Experience of P3M Association." In *Islam, Reproductive Health, and Women's Rights*, ed. Zainah Anwar and Rashidah Abdullah, 199–221. Kuala Lumpur: Sisters in Islam.

Marecek, Jeanne. 2000. "'Am I a Woman in These Matters?' Notes on Sinhala Nationalism and Gender in Sri Lanka." In *Gender Ironies of Nationalism: Sexing the Nation*, ed. Tamar Mayer, 139–62. New York: Routledge.

Mas'udi, Masdar. 1997. *Islam dan Hak-Hak Reproduksi Peremupan: Dialog Fiqih Pemberdayaan* [*Islam and Women's Reproductive Rights: A Dialogue of the Islamic Jurisprudence of Empowerment*]. Bandung: Mizan.

McLelland, Mark J. 2002. "Kamingu Auto: Homosexuality and Popular Culture in Japan." *IIAS* [*International Institute for Asian Studies*] *Newsletter* 29:7.

Miller, Barbara D. 2001. "Female-Selective Abortion in Asia: Patterns, Policies, and Debates." *American Anthropolgist* 103(4): 1083–95.

Mohanty, Chandra. 1991. "Under Western Eyes: Feminist Scholarship and Colonial Discourses." In *Third World Women and the Politics of Feminism*, ed. Chandra Mohanty, Ann Russo, and Lourdes Torres, 51–80. Bloomington: Indiana University Press.

Mookherjee, Nayanika. 2003. "Ethical Issues Concerning Representation of Narratives of Sexual Violence in 1971." www.drishtipat.org/1971.

Morris, Rosalind. 1994. "Three Sexes and Four Sexualities: Redressing the Discourses on Gender and Sexuality in Contemporary Thailand." *positions: east asia cultures critique* 2(1): 15-43.

Murphey, Rhoads. 1996. *A History of Asia*, 2nd ed. New York: HarperCollins.

Nanda, Serena. 1990. *Neither Man nor Woman: The Hijras of India*. Belmont: Wadsworth.

—. 1993. "Hijras: An Alternative Sex and Gender Role in India." In *Third Sex, Third Gender: Beyond Sexual Dimorphism in Culture and History*, ed. Gilbert Herdt, 373–417. New York: Zone.

—. 2000. *Gender Diversity: Cross-Cultural Variations*. Long Grove, IL: Waveland.

Oetomo, Dede. 1996. "Gender and Sexual Orientation in Indonesia." In *Fantasizing the Feminine in Indonesia*, ed. Laurie Sears, 259–69. Durham: Duke University Press.

Ong, Aihwa. 1987. *Spirits of Resistance and Capitalist Discipline: Factory Women in Malaysia*. Albany: State University of New York Press.

—. 1991. "The Gender and Labor Politics of Post-Modernity." *Annual Review of Anthropology* 20:279–309.

—. 1999. *Flexible Citizenship: The Cultural Logics of Transnationality*. Durham: Duke University Press.

Onishi, Norimitsu. 2004. "A Crash Course in Tradition for Modern Korean Brides." *New York Times*, June 25.

Ortner, Sherry B. 1996. "Gender Hegemonies." In *Making Gender: The Politics and Erotics of Culture*, 139–72. Boston: Beacon Press.

————. 1999. *Life and Death on Mount Everest: Sherpas and Himalayan Mountaineering*. Princeton: Princeton University Press.

Papanek, Hannah. 1979. "Family Status Production: The 'Work' and 'Nonwork' of Women." *Signs* 4(4): 775–81.

Peletz, Michael G. 1995. "Neither Reasonable nor Responsible: Contrasting Representations of Masculinity in a Malay Society." In *Bewitching Women, Pious Men: Gender and Body Politics in Southeast Asia*, ed. Aihwa Ong and Michael G. Peletz. 76–123. Berkeley: University of California Press.

————. 1996. *Reason and Passion: Representations of Gender in a Malay Society*. Berkeley: University of California Press.

————. 2002. *Islamic Modern: Religious Courts and Cultural Politics in Malaysia*. Princeton: Princeton University Press.

————. 2006. "Transgenderism and Gender Pluralism in Southeast Asia since Early Modern Times." *Current Anthropology* 47(2): 309–25, 333–40.

————. Forthcoming. *Gender Pluralism: Southeast Asia since Early Modern Times*. New York: Routledge.

Pelzel, John. 1970. "Japanese Kinship: A Comparison." In *Family and Kinship in Chinese Society*, ed. Maurice Freedman, 227–48. Stanford: Stanford University Press.

Pelzer, Kristin. 1993. "Socio-cultural Dimensions of Renovation in Vietnam: *Doi Moi* as Dialogue and Transformation in Gender Relations." In *Reinventing Vietnamese Socialism: Doi Moi in Comparative Perspective*, ed. William Turley and Mark Selden, 309–35. Boulder: Westview.

Pflugfelder, Gregory. 1999. *Cartographies of Desire: Male-Male Sexualities in Japanese Discourse, 1600–1950*. Berkeley: University of California Press.

Phillimore, Peter. 1991. "Unmarried Women and the Dhaula Dhar: Celibacy and Social Control in Northwest India." *Journal of Anthropological Research* 47(3): 331–50.

Pike, Linnet. 2002. "Sex Work and Socialization in a Moral World: Conflict and Change in Badi Communities in Western Nepal." In *Coming of Age in South and Southeast Asia: Youth, Courtship, and Sexuality*, ed. Lenore Manderson and Pranee Liamputtong, 228–48. Richmond, Surrey: Curzon.

Pradhan. G. 1992. "Road to Bombay: In Relation to the Trafficking and Selling of Women and Children." *Voice of Child Workers* 15–16:41–49.

Proschan, Frank. 1998. "Filial Piety and Non-Procreative Male-to-Male Sex among Vietnamese." Paper presented at the annual meetings of the American Anthropological Association.

PuruShotam, Nirmala. 1998. "Between Compliance and Resistance: Women and the Middle-Class Way of Life in Singapore." In *Gender and Power in Affluent Asia*, ed. Krishna Sen and Maila Stivens, 127–66. London: Routledge.

Rabinowtiz, Gavin. 2007. "Hearts on Fire in India: Religious Hard-liners Attack Valentine's Events." *Atlanta Journal Constitution*, February 15.

Raheja, Gloria G., and Ann G. Gold. 1994. *Listen to the Heron's Words: Reimagining Gender and Kinship in North India*. Berkeley: University of California Press.

Rappaport, Roy. 1999. *Ritual and Religion in the Making of Humanity*. New York: Cambridge University Press.

Reddy, Gayatri. 2005. *With Respect to Sex: Negotiating Hijra Identity in South India*. Chicago: University of Chicago Press.

Reid, Anthony. 1988. *Southeast Asia in the Age of Commerce, 1450–1680*. Vol. 1: *The Land below the Winds*. New Haven: Yale University Press.

———. 1993. *Southeast Asia in the Age of Commerce, 1450–1680*. Vol. 2: *Expansion and Crisis*. New Haven: Yale University Press.

Robertson, Jennifer. 1998. *Takarazuka: Sexual Politics and Popular Culture in Modern Japan*. Berkeley: University of California Press.

Roscoe, Will. 1996. "Priests of the Goddess: Gender Transgression in Ancient Religion." *History of Religions* 35(3): 195–230.

———. 1998. *Changing Ones: Third and Fourth Genders in Native North America*. New York: St. Martin's.

Rubin, Gayle. 1984. "Thinking Sex: Notes for a Radical Theory of the Politics of Sexuality." In *Pleasure and Danger: Exploring Female Sexuality*, ed. Carole Vance, 267–319. Boston: Routledge and Kegan Paul.

Ryang, Sonia. 2000. "Gender in Oblivion: Women in the Democratic People's Republic of Korea (North Korea)." *African and Asian Studies* 35(3): 323–49.

Said, Edward. 1988. "Foreword". In *Selected Subaltern Studies*, ed. Ranajit Guha and Gayatri Chakravorty Spivak, v–x. New York: Oxford University Press.

Sanday, Peggy. 1981. *Female Power and Male Dominance: On the Origins of Sexual Inequality*. Cambridge: Cambridge University Press.

———. 1990. *Fraternity Gang Rape: Sex, Brotherhood, and Privilege on Campus*. New York: New York University Press.

Sang, Tze-Ian D. 2003. *The Emerging Lesbian: Female Same-Sex Desire in Modern China*. Chicago: University of Chicago Press.

Sankar, Andrea. 1986. "Sisters and Brothers, Lovers and Enemies: Marriage Resistance in Southern Kwangtung." In *The Many Faces of Homosexuality: Anthropological Approaches to Homosexual Behavior*, ed. Evelyn Blackwood, 69–81. New York: Harrington Park.

Scott, James. 1985. *Weapons of the Weak: Everyday Forms of Peasant Resistance*. New Haven: Yale University Press.

Seabrook, Jeremy. 2001. *Travels in the Skin Trade: Tourism and the Sex Industry.* 2nd ed. London: Pluto.

Shah, Nayan. 2001. *Contagious Divide: Epidemics and Race in San Francisco's Chinatown.* Berkeley: University of California Press.

Sinnott, Megan. 2004. *Toms and Dees: Transgender Identity and Female Same-Sex Relationships in Thailand.* Honolulu: University of Hawai'i Press.

Skidmore, Monique. 2004. *Karaoke Fascism: Burma and the Politics of Fear.* Philadelphia: University of Pennsylvania Press.

Smith-Hefner, Nancy. 1999. *Khmer American: Identity and Moral Education in a Diasporic Community.* Berkeley: University of California Press.

Somswasdi, Virada. 2004. "Legalization of Prostitution in Thailand: A Challenge to Feminism and Societal Conscience." Paper presented at the Cornell Law School Berger International Speaker Series, March 9.

Spiro, Melford. 1997. *Gender Ideology and Psychological Reality: An Essay on Cultural Reproduction.* New Haven: Yale University Press.

Strassler, Karen. 2004. "Gendered Visibilities and the Dream of Transparency: The Chinese-Indonesian Rape Debate in Post-Suharto Indonesia." *Gender and History* 16(3): 689–725.

Tamanoi, Mariko Asano. 1990. "Women's Voices: Their Critique of the Anthropology of Japan." *Annual Review of Anthropology* 19: 17–37.

Tambiah, Stanley J. 1989. "*Bridewealth and Dowry* Revisited: The Position of Women in Sub-Saharan Africa and North India." *Current Anthropology* 30(4): 413–35.

———. 1992. *Buddhism Betrayed? Religion, Politics, and Violence in Sri Lanka.* Chicago: University of Chicago Press.

Topley, Marjorie. 1959. "Immigrant Chinese Female Servants and Their Hostels in Singapore." *Man* 59: 213–15.

Tsing, Anna. 2005. *Friction: An Ethnography of Global Connection.* Princeton: Princeton University Press.

Van Esterik, Penny. 2000. *Materializing Thailand.* Oxford: Berg.

Vaughn, James C. 2006. "The Culture of the Bohemian Grove: The Dramaturgy of Power." *Michigan Sociological Review* 20: 85–123.

Vervoorn, Aat. 2002. *Re Orient: Change in Asian Societies.* 2nd ed. Melbourne: Oxford University Press.

Warren, James. [1986] 2003. *Rickshaw Coolie: A People's History of Singapore, 1880-1940.* Singapore: Singapore University Press.

———. 1993. *Ah Ku and Karayuki-San: Prostitution in Singapore, 1870–1940.* Singapore: Oxford University Press.

Wilchins, Riki. 1997. *Read My Lips: Sexual Subversion and the End of Gender.* Ithaca: Firebrand.

Williams, Raymond. 1977. *Marxism and Literature*. Oxford: Oxford University Press.

Wolf, Diane. 1990. "Daughters, Decisions, and Domination: An Empirical and Conceptual Critique of Household Strategies." *Development and Change* 21: 43–74.

———. 1992. *Factory Daughters: Gender, Household Dynamics, and Rural Industrialization in Java*. Berkeley: University of California Press.

World Health Organization. 2007. Global Health Atlas. http://www.who.int/globalatlas/default.asp.

Yardley, Jim. 2006. "New Estimate in China Finds Fewer AIDS Cases." *New York Times*, January 26.

Suggestions for Further Reading

Abelmann, Nancy. 2003. *The Melodrama of Mobility: Women, Talk, and Class in Contemporary South Korea*. Honolulu: University of Hawai'i Press.

Abelove, Henry, Michele Barale, and David Halperin, eds. 1993. *The Lesbian and Gay Studies Reader*. New York: Routledge.

Afkhami, Mahnaz, ed. 1995. *Faith and Freedom: Women's Human Rights in the Muslim World*. Syracuse: Syracuse University Press.

Agnes, Flavia. 1999. *Law and Gender Inequality: The Politics of Women's Rights in India*. New Delhi: Oxford University Press.

Alexander, M. Jacqui, and Chandra T. Mohanty, eds. 1997. *Feminist Genealogies, Colonial Legacies, Democratic Futures*. New York: Routledge.

Allison, Anne. 1994. *Nightwork: Sexuality, Pleasure, and Corporate Masculinity in a Tokyo Hostess Club*. Chicago. University of Chicago Press.

———. 1996. *Permitted and Prohibited Desires: Mothers, Comics, and Censorship in Japan*. Boulder: Westview.

Andaya, Barbara W. 2006. *The Flaming Womb: Repositioning Women in Early Modern Southeast Asia*. Honolulu: University of Hawai'i Press.

Argenti-Pillen, Alex. 2003. *Masking Terror: How Women Contain Violence in Southern Sri Lanka*. Philadelphia: University of Pennsylvania Press.

Bernstein, Gail. 2005. *Isami's House: Three Centuries of a Japanese Family*. Berkeley: University of California Press.

Bernstein, Gail, Andrew Gordon, and Kate Nakai, eds. 2005. *Public Spheres, Private Lives in Modern Japan, 1600–1950: Essays in Honor of Albert Craig*. Cambridge: Cambridge University Press.

Blackwood, Evelyn, and Saskia Wieringa, eds. 1999. *Female Desires: Same-Sex Relations and Transgender Practices across Cultures*. New York: Columbia University Press.

Bleys, Rudi. 1995. *The Geography of Perversion: Male-to-Male Sexual Behaviour Outside the West and the Ethnographic Imagination, 1750–1918*. New York: New York University Press.

Boellstorff, Tom. 2005. *The Gay Archipelago: Sexuality and Nation in Indonesia*. Princeton: Princeton University Press.

Brenner, Suzanne. 1998. *The Domestication of Desire: Women, Wealth, and Modernity in Java*. Princeton: Princeton University Press.

Butalia, Urvashi. 2000. *The Other Side of Silence: Voices from the Partition of India*. Durham: Duke University Press.

Butler, Judith. 1990. *Gender Trouble: Feminism and the Subversion of Identity*. New York: Routledge.

Cannell, Fenella. 1999. *Power and Intimacy in the Christian Philippines*. Cambridge: Cambridge University Press.

Carsten, Janet. 1997. *The Heat of the Hearth: The Process of Kinship in a Malay Fishing Community*. Oxford: Oxford University Press.

Chatterjee, Partha. 1994. *The Nation and Its Fragments: Colonial and Postcolonial Histories*. Princeton: Princeton University Press.

Chin, Christine. 1998. *In Service and Servitude: Foreign Female Domestic Workers and the Malaysian "Modernity" Project*. New York: Columbia University Press.

Cohen, Lawrence. 1998. *No Aging in India: Alzheimer's, the Bad Family, and Other Modern Things*. Berkeley: University of California Press.

Collier, Jane F., and Sylvia J. Yanagisako, eds. 1987. *Gender and Kinship: Essays toward a Unified Analysis*. Stanford: Stanford University Press.

Connell, R.W. 1995. *Masculinities*. Berkeley: University of California Press.

Constable, Nicole. 1997. *Maid to Order in Hong Kong: Stories of Filipina Workers*. Ithaca: Cornell University Press.

Crompton, Louis. 2003. *Homosexuality and Civilization*. Cambridge: Harvard University Press.

Das, Veena, Arthur Kleinman, Mamphela Ramphele, and Pamela Reynolds, eds. 2000. *Violence and Subjectivity*. Berkeley: University of California Press.

Despeux, Catherine, and Livia Kohn. 2003. *Women in Daoism*. Cambridge: Three Pine.

Drummond, Lisa, and Helle Rydstrom, eds. 2004. *Gender Practices in Contemporary Vietnam*. Honolulu: University of Hawai'i Press.

El-Rouayheb, Khaled. 2005. *Before Homosexuality in the Arab-Islamic World, 1500-1800*. Chicago: University of Chicago Press.

Eng, David L., and Alice Y. Hom, eds. 1998. *Q & A: Queer in Asian America*. Philadelphia: Temple University Press.

Faure, Bernard. 1998. *The Red Thread: Buddhist Approaches to Sexuality*. Princeton: Princeton University Press.

Flueckiger, Joyce B. 2006. *In Amma's Healing Room: Gender and Vernacular Islam in South India*. Bloomington: Indiana University Press.

Garcia, J. Neil C. 1996. *Philippine Gay Culture: The Last Thirty Years*. Quezon City: University of the Philippines Press.

Ginsburg, Faye, and Rayna Rapp, eds. 1995. *Conceiving the New World Order: The Global Politics of Reproduction*. Berkeley: University of California Press.

Goody, Jack. 1996. *The East in the West*. Cambridge: Cambridge University Press.

Graham, Sharyn. 2007. *Challenging Gender Norms: Five Genders among Bugis in Indonesia*. Belmont, CA.: Wadsworth.

Haeri, Shahla. 2002. *No Shame for the Sun: Lives of Professional Pakistani Women*. Syracuse: Syracuse University Press.

Herdt, Gilbert, ed. 1993. *Third Sex, Third Gender: Beyond Sexual Dimorphism in Culture and History*. New York: Zone.

Hyun, Theresa. 2003. *Writing Women in Korea: Translation and Feminism in the Colonial Period*. Honolulu: University of Hawai'i Press.

Ireson-Doolittle, Carol, and Geraldine Moreno-Black. 2004. *The Lao: Gender, Power, and Livelihood*. Boulder: Westview.

Jackson, Peter A., and Nerida M. Cook, eds. 1999. *Genders and Sexualities in Modern Thailand*. Chiang Mai: Silkworm.

Jackson, Peter A., and Gerard Sullivan, eds. 1999. *Lady Boys, Tom Boys, Rent Boys: Male and Female Homosexualities in Contemporary Thailand*. New York: Harrington Park.

Johnston, William. 2005. *Geisha, Harlot, Strangler, Star: A Woman, Sex, and Morality in Modern Japan*. New York: Columbia University Press.

Jones, Gavin, and Kamalini Ramdas, eds. 2004. *(Un)Tying the Knot: Ideal and Reality in Asian Marriage*. Honolulu: University of Hawai'i Press.

Karim, Wazir Jahan. 1992. *Women and Culture: Between Malay Adat and Islam*. Boulder: Westview Press.

Karim, Wazir Jahan, ed. 1995. *'Male' and 'Female' in Developing Southeast Asia*. Oxford: Berg.

Keeler, Ward. 2005. "'But Princes Jump!' Performing Masculinity in Mandalay." In *Burma at the Turn of the Twenty-first Century*, ed. Monique Skidmore, 206–28. Honolulu: University of Hawai'i Press.

Kendall, Laurel. 1985. *Shamans, Housewives, and Other Restless Spirits: Women in Korean Ritual Life*. Honolulu: University of Hawai'i Press.

Kendall, Laurel, ed. 2002. *Under Construction: The Gendering of Modernity, Class, and Consumption in the Republic of Korea*. Honolulu: University of Hawai'i Press.

Kim, Elaine, and Chungnoo Choi. 1998. *Dangerous Women: Gender and Korean Nationalism*. New York: Routledge.

Laderman, Carol. 1983. *Wives and Midwives: Childbirth and Nutrition in Rural Malaysia*. Berkeley: University of California Press.

———. 1991. *Taming the Wind of Desire: Psychology, Medicine, and Aesthetics in Malay Shamanistic Performance*. Berkeley: University of California Press.

Lamb, Sarah. 2000. *White Saris and Sweet Mangoes: Aging, Gender, and Body in North India*. Berkeley: University of California Press.

Lebra, Takie. 1984. *Japanese Women: Constraint and Fulfillment.* Honolulu: University of Hawai'i Press.

———. 2006. *Identity, Gender, and Status in Japan.* Honolulu: University of Hawai'i Press.

Lilja, Mona. 2006. *Power, Resistance, and Women Politicians in Cambodia: Discourses of Emancipation.* Honolulu: University of Hawai'i Press.

Lock, Margaret. 1993. *Encounters with Aging: Mythologies of Menopause in Japan and North America.* Berkeley: University of California Press.

Loos, Tamara. 2005. "Sex in the Inner City: The Fidelity between Sex and Politics in Siam." *Journal of Asian Studies* 64(4): 881–909.

Lopez, Donald S., ed. 2002. *Religions of Asia in Practice: An Anthology.* Princeton: Princeton University Press.

Louie, Kam, and Morris Low, eds. 2003. *Asian Masculinities: The Meaning and Practice of Manhood in China and Japan.* London: RoutledgeCurzon.

Manderson, Lenore, and Margaret Jolly, eds. 1997. *Sites of Desire, Economies of Pleasure: Sexualities in Asia and the Pacific.* Chicago: University of Chicago Press.

Mann, Susan, ed. 2004. *Women and Gender Relations: Perspectives on Asia.* Ann Arbor: Association for Asian Studies.

McClintock, Anne, Aamir Mufti, and Ella Shohat, eds. 1997. *Dangerous Liaisons: Gender, Nation, and Postcolonial Perspectives.* Minneapolis: University of Minnesota Press.

McLelland, Mark. 2000. *Male Homosexuality in Modern Japan: Cultural Myths and Social Realities.* Richmond, UK: Curzon.

Menon, Ritu, and Kamla Bhasin. 1998. *Borders and Boundaries: Women in India's Partition.* New Brunswick, NJ: Rutgers University Press.

Miller, Barbara D. 1981. *The Endangered Sex: Neglect of Female Children in Rural North India.* Ithaca: Cornell University Press.

Mills, Mary Beth. 1999. *Thai Women in the Global Labor Force: Consuming Desires, Contested Selves.* New Brunswick, NJ: Rutgers University Press.

Mohanty, Chandra, Ann Russo, and Lourdes Torres, eds. 1991. *Third World Women and the Politics of Feminism.* Bloomington: Indiana University Press.

Molony, Barbara, and Kathleen Uno, eds. 2005. *Gendering Modern Japanese History.* Cambridge: Harvard University Press.

Moore, Henrietta. 1994. *A Passion for Difference: Essays in Anthropology and Gender.* Bloomington: Indiana University Press.

Murray, Stephen O., and Will Roscoe, eds. 1997. *Islamic Homosexualities: Culture, History, and Literature.* New York: New York University Press.

Narayan, Kirin. 1989. *Storytellers, Saints, and Scoundrels: Folk Narrative in Hindu Religious Teaching.* Philadelphia: University of Pennsylvania Press.

———. 1997. *Mondays on the Dark Night of the Moon: Himalayan Foothill Folktales*. New York: Oxford University Press.

Ng, Cecilia, Maznah Mohamad, and tan beng hui. 2006. *Feminism and the Women's Movement in Malaysia: An Unsung (R)evolution*. London: Routledge.

Nobue, Suzuki. 2003. "Transgressing 'Victims': Reading Narratives of 'Filipina Brides' in Japan." *Critical Asian Studies* 35(3): 399–420.

Obeyesekere, Gananath. 1981. *Medusa's Hair: An Essay on Personal Symbols and Religious Experience*. Chicago: University of Chicago Press.

Ong, Aihwa. 2006. *Neoliberalism as Exception: Mutations in Citizenship and Sovereignty*. Durham: Duke University Press.

Ong, Aihwa, and Michael G. Peletz, eds. 1995. *Bewitching Women, Pious Men: Gender and Body Politics in Southeast Asia*. Berkeley: University of California Press.

O'Flaherty, Wender Doniger. 1980. *Women, Androgynes, and Other Mythical Beasts*. Chicago: University of Chicago Press.

O'Neill, John. 1985. *Five Bodies: The Human Shape of Modern Society*. Ithaca: Cornell University Press.

Ortner, Sherry B., and Harriet Whitehead, eds. 1981. *Sexual Meanings: The Cultural Construction of Gender and Sexuality*. Cambridge: Cambridge University Press.

Parker, Andrew, Mary Russo, Doris Sommer, and Patricia Yeager, eds. 1992. *Nationalisms and Sexualities*. New York: Routledge.

Pathak, Zakia, and Rajeswari Sunder Rajan. 1989. "Shahbano." *Signs* 14(3): 559–82.

Patton, Laurie L., ed. 2002. *Jewels of Authority: Women and Textual Tradition in Hindu India*. New York: Oxford University Press.

Roberson, James E. and Nobue Suzuki, eds. 2003. *Men and Masculinities in Contemporary Japan: Dislocating the Salaryman Doxa*. London: RoutledgeCurzon.

Rofel, Lisa. 1999. *Other Modernities: Gendered Yearnings in China after Socialism*. Berkeley: University of California Press.

Said, Edward. 1978. *Orientalism*. New York: Pantheon.

Sand, Jordan. 2004. *House and Home in Modern Japan: Architecture, Domestic Space, and Bourgeois Culture, 1880–1930*. Cambridge: Harvard University Press.

Sears, Laurie, ed. 1996. *Fantasizing the Feminine in Indonesia*. Durham: Duke University Press.

Sen, Krishna, and Maila Stivens, eds. 2002. *Gender and Power in Affluent Asia*. London: Routledge.

Stivens, Maila. 1996. *Matriliny and Modernity: Sexual Politics and Social Change in Rural Malaysia*. Sydney: Allen and Unwin.

Stoler, Ann L. 1995. *Race and the Education of Desire: Foucault's History of Sexuality and the Colonial Order of Things*. Durham: Duke University Press.

———. 2002. *Carnal Knowledge and Imperial Power: Race and the Intimate in Colonial Rule*. Berkeley: University of California Press.

Tamanoi, Mariko. 1998. *Under the Shadow of Nationalism: Politics and Poetics of Rural Japanese Women*. Honolulu: University of Hawai'i Press.

Trawick, Margaret. 1990. *Notes on Love in a Tamil Family*. Berkeley: University of California Press.

Turner, Bryan. 1996. *The Body and Society: Explorations in Social Theory*, 2nd ed. Oxford: Basil Blackwell.

Van Esterik, Penny, ed. 1996. *Women of Southeast Asia*, Rev. ed. Dekalb: Center for Southeast Asian Studies, Northern Illinois University.

Vanita, Ruth, ed. 2002. *Queering India: Same-Sex Love and Eroticism in Indian Culture and Society*. New York: Routledge.

Visweswaran, Kamala. 1994. *Fictions of Feminist Ethnography*. Minneapolis: University of Minnesota Press.

Weston, Kath. 1998. *Long Slow Burn: Sexuality and Social Science*. New York: Routledge.

Wilson, Ara. 2004. *The Intimate Economies of Bangkok: Tomboys, Tycoons, and Avon Ladies in the Global City*. Berkeley: University of California Press.

Wolf, Margery. 1972. *Women and the Family in Rural Taiwan*. Stanford: Stanford University Press.

———. 1992. *A Thrice-Told Tale: Feminism, Postmodernism, and Ethnographic Responsibility*. Stanford: Stanford University Press.